GREAT RAILWAY
JOURNEYS
OF THE WORLD

MICHAEL FRAYN   LUDOVIC KENNEDY

MILES KINGTON   MICHAEL PALIN

ERIC ROBSON   BRIAN THOMPSON

MICHAEL WOOD

GREAT RAILWAY JOURNEYS OF THE WORLD

E. P. DUTTON, INC.   NEW YORK

PICTURE CREDITS

Amtrak, Washington, D.C. (print from *Mars,* London), page 99. *Australian News & Information Service,* page 75 (Douglas McNaughton). *Barnaby's Picture Library,* pages 6 (E. Norman Issott), 15 (R. Dalmaine), 133 (G.E.A. Fiddes), 145 (B. Wray), 148 (Allan S. Campbell), 151 (E.J. Goodall), 170 (G.D. Lindley). *J. Allan Cash,* page 8. *Brian James,* pages 37 and 51. *Millbrook House Ltd,* pages 32 (C.J. Allen Collection), 55; 61 and 63 (both C.J. Allen Collection), 109, 135, 143, and 169 (Osterreichische Bundesbahnen), and 172. *Brian Morrison,* page 154. *Tony Morrison,* pages 111, 124, and 127. *Peter Newark's Western Americana,* pages 95 and 100. *The Oakland Museum,* page 98. *Pennsylvania Railroad—* George Pins Collection, pages 82/83. *Eric Robson,* page 176. *Santa Fe Railway,* page 87. *Swiss National Tourist Office,* pages 161, 163, 164, and 167. *U.S.P.G.,* page 41. *Utah State Historical Society,* page 97.

First published in the U.K. in 1981

First published in the United States in 1982 by E.P. Dutton, Inc., 2 Park Avenue, New York, N.Y. 10016

Library of Congress Catalog Card Number: 82-71251
ISBN: 0-525-24152-3

10 9 8 7 6 5 4 3 2 1

Contents

CONTENTS

Introduction

ROGER LAUGHTON

There are two groups of rail buffs. The smaller group is the more visible. Its members stand at the end of station platforms, notebook in hand, waiting for passing Deltics. Michael Palin is the apotheosis of this type. With his Ian Allan handbook, he could have been discovered on sunny summer evenings in 1955 dedicatedly train-spotting at Sheffield Midland. When he revealed his passion for trains to a 1980 television audience, the reaction was immediate and enthusiastic. Millions shared his sense of pride in the greatest railway system in the world and remembered their own childhood preoccupation with engines and engine-drivers. For many, like Michael, that obsession has never left them.

But there is another group of railway lovers. Its members cannot tell a Black Five from a Lamborghini. They are not trainspotters, but train travellers. Their qualification for membership is a desire to travel by train whenever they have the choice. This book is mainly for them.

Thirty years ago, there was no alternative to railway travel. Long-distance journeys, even across continents, meant travelling by train. Ludovic Kennedy did not choose to cross America by rail when he and his wife went from New York to Hollywood in 1950. It was the only way to go. Nowadays, such is the pace of change, you have to be old, eccentric or a tourist to cross the United States by train. The poor take the bus, the rich fly. Jumbo jets and freeways have almost eliminated the crack expresses which once bound America together; even romantics like me accept the sad reality that only tourist trains will take the great transcontinental route once today's rolling-stock wears out.

But, elsewhere in the world, passenger trains are by no means in decline. In Britain, where it all began, more people are taking the train now than a decade ago. In South Africa the Blue Train, most luxurious of all the world's passenger services as Mike Wood discovered, now sometimes runs not twice, but three times a week. At the heart of this revival there is a simple truth. People like travelling by train even when it is more expensive and less convenient than driving or flying.

One writer in particular speaks for those of us who refused to accept the Railway Age had ended. He did not make a journey for the BBC. But something Paul Theroux wrote in his account of a journey across Asia, *The Great Railway Bazaar*, served as a text during the making of the TV programmes *Great Railway Journeys of the World*. He wrote, 'I sought trains, I found passengers.' Our travellers, too, brought back the same story. If you want to join the least exclusive club in the world, buy a second-class train ticket and meet your fellow travellers. I believe this lay behind the warmth of the response to the television films, screened by the BBC in the autumn of 1980. You may be alone on a train – but you are rarely lonely. These accounts of the train journeys are not primarily about the history of railways, although that history is everywhere visible to those who want to find it. Nor are they about the future of railways, although the energy crises of the 1970s have confounded experts' predictions. Essentially they are about what it is like to travel through today's world at a pace and in a manner suited to the human condition. Whoever heard of train lag?

Today we are often frightened by technological progress – usually for excellent reasons. But, if our experience of riding the world's trains counts for anything, it demonstrates that people's worst fears about progress are sometimes unfounded. The Victorians, more optimistic than we are about the impact of science, celebrated their railway-building achievements with great confidence and a notable lack of embarrassment. For them railways meant an advance, both geographical and spiritual.

It is the same today in much of the so-called third world. Try telling a newly-qualified engineer in Zimbabwe that railways bring industrialisation, and industrialisation brings misery. When the railroad is the highway to national prosperity, few stand in its way. Until the nation-state itself declines, railways will continue to play a prime role in forming national unity. Michael Frayn's witty description of the genesis of the Indian Pacific, the train that carried him across the Australian desert, is a case in point.

But the pieces in this book are not really about the links between government and railways. The only time political events played an explicit part in these journeys was when our film crew arrived in Bolivia. Miles Kington and his colleagues crossed Lake Titicaca from Peru on the very day the then government was overthrown in a military coup. The journey ended, not as planned in La Paz, but at a small wayside station called Viacha.

The Bolivian mishap was an exception. Day-by-day experience of train travel during normal times brought my colleagues into close contact, not with politicians, but with the international fraternity of railwaymen. Stationmasters in India, signalmen in the Yorkshire Dales, barmen on the Broadway, engineers in the outback – it was a privilege to meet them. Everywhere we found them dedicated to the efficient running of their railroad, with (it has to be said) varying degrees of success. After you have read Brian Thompson's account of his leisurely journey through southern India you will not forget the charm and courtesy of the railway employees he met as he meandered towards Cochin.

I must thank my colleagues, too many of them to mention individually by name, who made the television films on which the travellers' tales in this book are based. We were not necessarily rail buffs when we started. Now, two years later, we know why Robert Louis Stevenson preferred to travel – usually by train – hopefully.

John Mason Brown, an American writer, put it another way. He wrote, 'The real joy to be had from riding trains begins where their usefulness ends.'

Roger Laughton

Executive producer

March 1981

INDIA

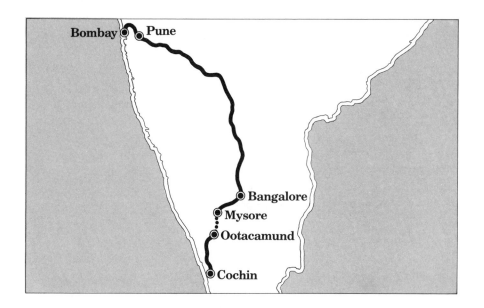

Deccan

BRIAN THOMPSON

For a long while, the train runs due south, and the sun is directly overheaɩ The shade temperature outside is in the hundreds. All the windows and the doors to the line are jammed wide open, and in the roof of the first-class accommodation, a battery of huge fans churns noisily. The seasoned passengers loll, or sleep; but to a European, travelling south in this stunning way is to go towards otherness. It is the direction of yearning, and even of oblivion. Seen from the window, a tawny countryside peels past, sometimes strewn with boulders, sometimes featureless and deserted. The train runs over huge, rumpled riverbeds with not a drop of water in them; it ploughs south, unwaveringly, and it takes all your imagination to remember that this plain was once a great prize of politics, a land fought over, laid waste to, and restored, for generation after generation of

1

princes. For only occasionally does a human figure appear – a young girl crouched in the shade of a stunted tree; a man in white walking resolutely out of the horizon down a perfectly straight road; a woman hoeing.

From time to time, the yellow emptiness gives way to valleys blessed with water. Then, there is a sudden shock of green – of rice, and palms, and little trees out on their own as if planted by some design, trimmed to a roundness by careful gardeners. And always, as this green appears, the train slows and the passengers wake. Where there is water in the Deccan, there is life. In every oasis of green, there is a railway station.

Those furnace-heat platforms! Immediately the train halts, sellers of fruit and water, tea, and the exquisite sweet coffee of India rush from the shade and serve the clamouring arms that hang from every window. Some passengers jump out and run to fill their water bottles, or douse small handkerchiefs under a tap and sponge their necks. A few grave men from the first class pace the platform or examine the line ahead with a borrowed professionalism. Around them, the station is frantic with shouts and the crying of babies. In the shade, unobtrusive, there sit the local people for whom this is theatre, an event, a celebration. They watch it all intently. A distraught man seizes on the unwary passenger with a tattered letter of recommendation yellow with age, something a chief clerk dictated long ago in some forgotten company in the city. A beggar is led by his grandson to each window in turn. He thrusts his hand in with the impatience of the blind.

Then suddenly – all too suddenly – a porter beats on a steel bar hanging from the rafters of the platform. There is a rush to board, an exasperated huff of steam, and the train fusses away. Looking back, I see only a scatter of people are left on the platform who resume moving with that languorous economy of gesture that is at the same time so appealing and so sad.

The journey I took through India by train was nothing very much, as to length or endurance. I did not (for example) go from the Himalayas to the foot of the subcontinent, where India dips its toe in two oceans and, it is said with wonder by those who have seen it, the sun rises and sets in the same place. I did not go even half that distance – and indeed, there were times when I wished only to stop, walk away from the tracks and set up some house or home and sit, and be still. India is no place to say 'I know *exactly* what I want to do' – something always intervenes and mocks that resolution. I travelled light, but still the greater part of my baggage was mental – my mind brought England along with me, and saw it shattered, sometimes with awe, and sometimes with dismay.

India is fashionable as a place to visit nowadays. But the history of Indian travel is littered with disparagements. You do not have to be there long to find out why. The very first visitors to India from Britain remarked on something that seemed to them to be very significant. It was noted with astonishment, and some condescension, that the peasant class of India paid not the slightest heed to the politics of the country. When the conquerors were a day's march away, the villagers buried their wealth and hid their women: after the storm had raged, they returned and tilled their fields. To the European mind, this fatalism made no sense. It was as though an intelligent and industrious people were somehow failing to come up to scratch.

I think if I had gone through India by any means other than a train, I too might have got a lot of things wrong. There is a good reason for this. From the very beginning of rail travel in the country, the greatest volume of passenger traffic was third class unreserved – village India. If you want to meet India – the reverberating bass note of the country – you must go by train. Day by day, year by year, the railways carry an immense population of people moving across its magnificent network, all of them unknowably motivated by considerations of business, of family, or religious fervour, or simple devotional obligation. It is not so much the trains and the track that seize your mind, but the passengers with whom you share the journey and their hundred destinations. W H Auden once proposed two natural images of man – in a city crowded with ghosts, or as a pilgrim on the road. I thought of this often on my journey, for it fits the newcomer's experience of India with an urgent accuracy. These are the only two landscapes.

A traveller comes to the country with an almost impossible weight on his back – the fact that we once believed, Britain as well as the rest of Europe, that India was ours to dispose of as we thought fit. This consideration was a tax on my ingenuity in planning the trip, for I wanted as far as possible to avoid the relics of the Raj. I wanted to make a journey that I could not prejudice by a background knowledge – say some classroom memory of Clive, or come to that, *The Bengal Lancers*. I wanted no wily Pathan, and no barrack-room ballads. The answer seemed to be to go south. And since I knew nothing of India, I was committed to going almost at random. India is such a large country. As I had hoped, the greatness of the journey was not in its route, but in moving in the restless tide of humanity that came so early to rail travel, and has accommodated it into its lifestyle ever since.

I decided to start the journey in Bombay. It was there in 1850 that the first sod of earth was turned for the construction of a railway. One can easily imagine it a not very auspicious moment. In the fever-ridden island which Bombay was then, the first sod of earth was much more likely to have been a spadeful of wet sand – and yet from that small beginning, the greatest rail system in all Asia arose. It was a notable curiosity of the day that when the Great India Peninsular Railway at last made its inaugural run, the governor of Bombay, the Commander-in-Chief, and the bishop all snubbed the occasion, having set off the night before by horseback and tonga for a sojourn in the hills 'in disregard of the memorable character of the occasion'. The *Bombay Times* was quite right to reprove them, for within only twenty years Bombay was connected to Calcutta *and* Madras and the whole peninsula had been spanned. It is said that when the first major obstacleonthe mainland presented itself – the Bhor Ghat, a mountain ridge which runs down the Western Coast like a giant palisade – 30,000 coolies died in forcing the way by tunnels, bridges and viaducts to the plateau of the Deccan. And yet from that moment, Bombay took on a new leadership. Today, its population stands at six million and it accounts for 15% of all industrial production.

All the same it turned out not to be my favourite city at all. Landing at the airport, a scent filled my nostrils so exactly that it is worth describing. It was exactly as if a firework display had just ended in a dank sea-cave – saltpetre, seaweed, woodsmoke, was all wrapped up in a midnight humidity that drenched me in sweat within a minute. I took a cab down to the narrow spit of land that was the original European quarter.

The first railway in India was commenced close to Apollo Bunder. In 1911 a monumental arch was erected there for the visit of the king-emperor. India Gate, as it was called, was built in such a fashion that George V could walk through to take symbolic possession of his lands and peoples. In the little park that was laid out then, there was later erected a more modest memorial, an equestrian statue of Sivaji, the Maratha warlord who finally expelled the Moguls from Central India. They make a nice contrast, and within the few square yards round and about the park you can find all the compressed ironies of a city, perhaps in particular an Indian city.

Apollo Bunder was the landing-place for all the nineteenth-century servants of the Queen, who were brought ashore in bumboats from ships anchored in the roads. Contemporary drawings show a strangely deserted scene. If there is a welcome in these pictures, it is a hidden one. Nowadays, there looms over the Gateway of India and Sivaji's statue a skyscraper hotel with a rooftop French restaurant and all the facilities required of the super-rich. And outside, from dawn until the very early hours of the next morning, are tribes of beggars, dope-dealers, hippies and hustlers, village people looking for work, all swirling and squabbling and sleeping on the pavements. A young boy explains the beggar economy: 'A German tourist, very nice, took me to his room. He gave me twenty rupees and told me to start a business.' The boy indicates a cardboard boxlid with half a dozen combs in it. His sister has rented a baby for the evening, a child she is hardly old enough to carry, and she staggers cheerfully to and fro, running after Western tourists, prodding the baby to make it cry. Round about, you can hear a babble of broken Italian, German, Russian and English; and, if you knew how to recognise them, half a dozen separate Indian tongues.

But Bombay, for all that it draws population from all over India, and prides itself on being the country's most cosmopolitan city, is not a handsome place. I don't at all mind acknowledging that I found it intimidating. There are said to be 16,000 taxis in Bombay, and on occasion they all seem to be coming down the same street. Now the one thing kept in good repair on a Bombay taxi is the horn, and no taxi-driver would dream of going more than a few yards without sounding it. The result is a day-long, huge and unrelenting cacophony. In any Western society, the sheer aggravation of so much unnecessary noise, so much pointless aggression, would lead to bloodshed. Yet in all the time I was in the city, I never saw an accident, and never once a quarrel or an argument. The noise and the diminution of human scale caused by the yellow cabs simply *is*, like the vultures wheeling overhead, or the emaciated figures in the gutter. And that seemed to me to be the point. If the people of Bombay don't appear to hear the cabs, they also don't appear to see the squalor. Nobody except the over-sensitive visitor does.

All of which disposed me, quite unfairly no doubt, to see Bombay almost immediately as a very good place to leave. I found myself thinking longingly of the India beyond the confines of the city. I knew as much about it as the most ignorant Victorian soldier, and yet I yearned to go, to take the railway and strike out into the unknown.

It happens that one of the greatest travel bargains in the world is the

Indrail Pass, which is only available to foreign tourists, and which provides unlimited travel for next to nothing. For as little as £30, the moment you have that despair and disgust with the city you can act upon it, going anywhere you will in what is still the fourth largest rail system in the world. I consulted the indispensable of rail travel, Murray's *Handbook for India, Burma and Ceylon*. (My edition was the fourth, of 1901, which caused amusement in Bombay, but I was greatly pleased to discover Jan Morris, whom I met by chance along the way, working from the third.) Murray's general notes were not encouraging. I had arrived at the very moment it was unwise to travel at all. 'April,' he noted, 'is as trying a month as any in the year.' His advice on striking out into the unknown was also daunting. 'If the traveller leaves the beaten track he must have a tiffin basket which should contain knives and forks and other simple fittings, and should always be kept furnished with potted meats, biscuits, some good spirits, and soda-water, which is good and cheap in India.' But if you were living in sybaritic bliss in Bombay, this marvellous book would send you away from it by the sheer weight of its curious detail; and the mood I was in, it acted like a trigger. With Murray under my arm, and only a very sketchy idea of Indian topography, I walked through the screaming streets to Stevens's great monument to Italian Gothic, Bombay Victoria Terminus.

The Foreign Visitors' Booking Clerk turned out to be a spruce South Indian called Mr Anantramiah. He is a diligent student of Dickens, an amateur photographer, and as far as his work goes, a complete railway encyclopedia. No question is too naïve for him to answer, at length and with exquisite formality. His memory for trains and timetables is astounding, and I tell him so. He regards me with composure.

'I am merely doing my duty. It is the duty of a railway employee to answer all questions correctly.'

'But you must get asked the same silly questions over and over again.'

'That is possible. But if I give the correct answer every time, am I not doing my duty?'

Mr Anantramiah belongs to a well-recognised élite. Over 5,000,000 people work for the railway system of India and the clerical divisions are to be measured in armies. As it was once in Britain, a job on the railways is a job for life – and compared to the life of the streets outside, which can seem unaccented and monotonous in its cruel opposition of the rich and poor, the railway system offers order and security. It is also the rich repository of

Victoria Railway Terminus, Bombay, famous
for its ornate Italian Gothic style

Tiffin boys arriving in Bombay on a suburban train. They collect hot dinners from office workers' homes and deliver them in insulated containers to their offices

that variant English that is comical and easy to deride, yet all the same a source of power for those who use it. A colleague of Mr Anantramiah's interrupts us.

'Which country are you from?'

'I'm from England.'

'You are on holiday?'

'Not exactly.'

'Ah,' he cries delightedly. 'Not exactly. Now what is this actually meaning?'

'More or less what it says.'

It is an accidental snub. The light of excitement dies in him, and he lowers his gaze to the ground. When he looks up it is to make amends.

'Now I am quite literally in the doghouse over this one,' he says mournfully.

Mr Anantramiah is made of sterner stuff. I explain to him that I wish to go south, and when he asks reasonably enough where I want to end up, and I say I don't know, no more than a beat in time passes. He adjusts his spectacles.

'Ah yes, I see. Well, that is very good. Then you may wish to go to Cochin, capital of Kerala. You can have an excursion there on the water which is like Paradise. That is what I have heard.'

'Have you been there?'

'Of course. It is very nice.'

'Is it like Paradise?'

He laughs. 'This is just an expression, perhaps,' he says good-humouredly.

So it was that I set off next morning on the Dadar Express, bound for Pune, the old Maratha capital and (after the railway had made the thing possible) the former summer quarters of the governor of Bombay. The journey lasts four hours. A diesel pulled us out with contemptuous ease through the slums, past hundreds of Indians squatting by the tracks, their shirts bunched over their stomachs, emptying their bowels with great concentration.

The Ghats, which presented such a challenge to the pioneers of the old GIPR, rise quite abruptly. They were once densely jungled. In clawing their way through the mountain to the tablelands at the top, the engineers constructed, on the most severe stretch, twenty-five tunnels, twenty-two bridges and eight viaducts. It says a lot for Victorian engineering that today the ascent seems unremarkable – so much so that no modern history of this rugged bit of railway has been written. An obliging passenger told me the story of the Mhowke Mullee viaduct. Completed in 1856, it had eight 50-foot arches, and spanned a ravine 150 feet deep. The villagers at the bottom complained to the railway officials that the structure was unsafe, since they could hear it groaning in pain. These petitions were ignored. Then one night, a year after completion and just after a train had passed, the whole lot fell into the ravine. The devastation of the viaduct was so complete that it could never be rebuilt – instead, by superhuman efforts, the coolies increased the rubble to the height of a massive embankment.

The goal of all this heroic enterprise was the Deccan plain. My first sight of it was awesome. Deccan means, simply, South. The basalt plateau stretches mile after mile for hundreds of miles, tawny, almost featureless and keening with heat. This plain was once the chequerboard of fierce politics, and in Sivaji's day his horsemen raised dust in every part of it. At its western edge is the Maratha capital, Pune – Poona of barrack-room legend. I arrived there hungry for history – and fell instead into the arms of a much more recent phenomenon.

There is an India which exists in the affection and even the awe of some young people who visit there: a better place, and a holier one, than the Europe or America they have left behind. This view of India has been characterised by the savagely ironical Indian writer Gita Mehta as The Search for Karma Cola. Well, you can go to Pune with any amount of intellectual curiosity, but the first thing that hits you when you walk out of the station is the amazing sight of hundreds of young Americans who are the disciples of Rajneesh Yogi. They are called 'oranges' from the clothes they wear, which are orange or cyclamen in colour. Round their necks they wear a portrait of the Bhagwan, suspended on a black bead necklace. They are very remarkable for their complacence.

In the comfortably air-conditioned lounge of a hotel, I met a Californian disciple of the Bhagwan. Many of his devotees were wandering about the swimming pool in distractingly tiny orange bikinis. The girl I was talking to had flown to Bombay from America, taken the same train as I had just done up the Bhor Ghat, and since then shopped around, as she put it, in the many self-discovery programmes of the ashram. She had not thought it necessary or even desirable to go to any other place in India.

'Are you going to go across to the ashram to catch discourse today? The Bhagwan's speaking and it's really beautiful. You ought to go, you know.'

'Does he speak in English?' I asked.

'This week's in Hindi.'

She did not speak Hindi, of course, and when I asked her how much that spoiled things, she flashed me a forgiving smile.

'You really don't have to understand a thing to know what's being said is beautiful.'

There was a curious sequel to this meeting. Later that summer I was in

France, in the Dordogne, looking for a holiday cottage we had rented. The roads narrowed and emptied of traffic, and we drove through the strangely seductive countryside that is so familiar and yet so foreign. The place was hard to find, but was signposted for us by the only two figures we had seen in a quarter of an hour. Sprawled by the side of the road were two 'oranges', their faces and bodies burned brown, and their clothes, in the holy colour of India, unkempt and filthy. Although they were together, this man and his woman, they were somehow also utterly apart. They lay against a bank of flowers, staring vacantly at the field opposite. A few hundred yards on was the house we were trying to find.

Away from India, the Bhagwan's disciples look a little forlorn; abject, even. But in Pune, they have a stage on which to play. The light and heat favour them; and they are in a society which, though it secretly reprehends them, is far too polite to say so. I asked several Pune residents what they thought of the Rajneeshi and they simply shook their heads in a modest negative.

The Bhagwan's injunction to his disciples is 'Do whatever is Easy: whatever is easy is right'. A few miles out on the plain, yet utterly unknown to the girl I met, is a landscape as fiercely difficult as any I have seen, where in 120° of heat the people creep like insects. There, oxcarts meander down roads made cloudy by even the slightest traffic, and the waters of a tank or a canal are like vaults of emerald, and not less precious. The basalt plain stretches away in depressing uniformity – out here a mile is as daunting to the imagination as a hundred miles. The sun beats on the thin skin of grass like a stick beating a cowed and mangy dog. Well over three-quarters of India lives in such an environment, amid the ruins of an ancient indigenous civilisation and with the superseded relics of alien empires scattered about. Forts, palaces, temples, whole cities are reverting, have long ago reverted, to so much rubble. They are what the local guidebooks call 'a melancholy bygone' and for me this same melancholy has already touched the 'oranges'.

That evening, waiting for the Madras Mail, the sun fell over the tracks like a huge poppy, and we, the passengers, a vast contradictory mass of humanity, watched and waited in patience for the arrival of the train. I was surprised and a bit alarmed to find myself the only European on the platform. As the short dusk raced in, the station glimmered white from the thin cotton suits of the older men. The air buzzed with a low-pitched, musical politeness. I felt as apt to describe all this as a falling stone, or a

feather. Tired, dishevelled, and reeling from the effect of the plains heat, I
wanted to get on that train, get to my compartment, and relax.

There now entered low comedy. According to the bookings I had made
with Mr Anantramiah, I would have the luxury of a compartment to
myself. The train drew in, and I found my name on a list pasted on the
carriage wall. I found my compartment. Inside, in a scatter of magazines
and orange peel, were four genial salesmen on their way home from a
promotional trip.

'I thought I would have the compartment to myself,' I said.

'Really?' one of the salesmen said archly. 'That would be unusual.'

It was nothing to write home about, that carriage. The livery of a first-
class reserved carriage is light and dark green. But you have to imagine it
coated in dust from the journey. The door to the corridor is made of light
steel and at night it is common to have it shut; when asleep, shuttered and
locked.

'Does someone come round with the bedding?'

They exchanged glances of the kind reserved for fools. Their spokesman
smiled gently.

'It is best to order bedding at the station before you leave. There is none
on the train.'

There was also one bunk too few, but this was not mentioned out of
mutual delicacy.

'Can I get something to eat on the train?'

'Certainly. A man will come round. You will tell him what you want to
eat, and he will telegraph ahead to the next station. They will prepare your
meal. You are on holiday?'

We fell to talking about cricket. After a while, I asked them if they had
ever met disciples of the Rajneesh. Their leader narrowed his eyes, as if
reviewing a great many cases.

'That one is not known,' he said diplomatically, 'but I am asking you
now: what do you think of Brian Close?'

It was a weird experience, the Night Mail. There are two sets of windows
in such carriages, as well as horizontal steel bars. Towards ten, the mesh
windows were pulled down and locked into position, and the glazed
windows likewise. It is still common – in fact it is an everyday news story –
that bandits hold up a train, strip the richer passengers and then make
their getaway by truck. We were nowhere near dacoit country, but all the
same, on a night journey you do find yourself about as open to the journey

as a pilchard in a tin. I lay up in the roof of the compartment, my head inches from the fan, undressed as far as having taken off my shoes. The train rattled away through the night.

You grow too quickly accustomed to distance in India. The Madras Mail goes from Bombay to Madras, in only twenty-four hours. During the night, I passed through Raichur, where the Madras Railway Company finally linked to the GIPR in 1871. As railway buffs know, there are three gauges to Indian railways – broad, metre, and narrow. The Mail runs on broad gauge and sweeps majestically across country that was disputed by princes and sultans for centuries. It crosses a plateau that for the first two centuries of British presence in India was almost completely unknown, connecting the great centre of British influence in one century – Madras – with its supplanter in the next. To have achieved a rail link between Bombay and Madras within only 21 years of the driving of the first spike on the subcontinent was a colossal piece of rail history. There was, for me, only one problem: I did not intend going to Madras.

Two of my travelling companions came from there. They were puzzled, and we chatted in the gloom.

'Madras is a very fine city.'

'Yes, but I don't want to see another city.'

'It is better place than Bombay.'

'All the same, I am going to get out at Guntakal.'

Suppressed peals of laughter.

'You must excuse the levity. But let me tell you one thing. At Guntakal, there is nothing. You will be getting off and finding nothing.'

'That was more or less the idea.'

More laughter, mixed this time with embarrassment.

Just after dawn the next day the train ran into the massive junction that is Guntakal. When my friends on the train said of the place there was nothing there, they meant of course there was no European-style accommodation. Nor is there. But at Guntakal the metre-gauge railway from Hyderabad crosses the broad-gauge tracks, and from this point on in the journey, all the trains I rode were pulled by steam.

In that sense, it is very much as train-spotters imagine heaven to be. Steam dominates the landscape. It huffs and shuffles, shrieks and blasts in and out of the sidings, and roars in the roof of the running sheds. Locos sidle up to children crossing the tracks on their way to school, or sigh luxuriously in the far distance, where the plumes from their smokestacks burst into a huge and empty horizon. The engines are like skaters or dancers, gliding and passing. A group of thirty or so men squatted in the early morning sunshine watching a couple of fitters tinker with an engine under repair. As far as I could tell, none of them worked for the railways. They were, absurdly, the replica of men in railway museums the world over.

In Western countries, the chances are we shall see this sort of thing again, as the oil dwindles and disappears. But Guntakal had another, greater meaning for me. There is a sense of pilgrim India about the place, an ordinariness that is not tired or defeated, but steady and purposeful. Once again, I was the only European on the whole station – and such an object of curiosity that I guessed also the first through there for a while. The rest of the milling passengers were villagers, without English, without wealth, and yet appealingly confident and assured. It was pointed out early by Marx how little of the money raised to fund railway expansion originated in India, or stayed there; but to be on Guntakal is to see *why* rail travel had its mass appeal. To be sure, there were businessmen, a few of them with suitcases dressed in cotton overalls, to be whipped off and used as dusters as the train reached its destination; but the majority of the travellers were humble people, toting sacks and cartons for luggage.

The station was a rich and complex anthology of travel. The Bangalore Express leaves just after nine. From dawn until time to board, those who have slept on the platform go through their ablutions, feed their children and themselves, repack or retie their belongings, talk to each other to the background accompaniment of steam whistles. I watched a man and his wife. She put on a sort of modesty tent over her clothes, and then wriggled out of her blouse and sari. She sat against the wall of a water trough, and little by little, from a steel drinking cup, he dashed her with water, head to toe, a cup at a time. Public affection is frowned upon in India, and it is not common to see, for example, a parent play with a child, unless that child is very young, or at the breast. Nor do you ever see sentiment between man and wife. The man bathing his wife did so with stiffbacked embarrassment, and hardly glanced at her. A European misses the gregarious quality in life: it comes as a surprise to realise that so many people are not in fact a crowd, but hundreds of quite separate units. It is only when the train boards that panic drives these gentle people into droves.

The Bangalore Express was if anything less clean than the Night Mail. Its

An XD class steam engine at Bangalore

carriages were coated with a fine red laterite dust, and I shared a compartment with a glistening cockroach. As we rattled south, the train seemed to shudder as it broached the heat. The land, and the people, were waiting for the rains. When that happens, the Deccan greens almost overnight. You only see a preview of *this* India in places where there is water. Then the rice seems to leap forward in its sharpness of colour, and you look out longingly on children washing down buffalo, or swimming in muddy lagoons. It is a seven-hour journey to Bangalore, and to while away the time, I spent part of it with Chief Train Guard Abdullah.

He wore the crisp white of the Southern Railway, and was a genial guide to a railwayman's life. Mr Abdullah retires in 1983, at the maximum of his salary scale.

'The pension is good. It is a very good *family* pension.'

'Are your sons in the service?'

He laughed richly. 'No, no. One son, he is doctor.'

'A doctor?'

'*Doctor*.'

He explained in passing that Bangalore was considered to be a second London, at any rate in the rainy season. The sky had grown quite overcast, and our conversation was punctuated by rolls of thunder. There was a brown tinge to the horizon.

'Will the monsoon come early this year?'

He shook his head. 'It's too hot. But today there may be some shower. In Bangalore.'

'The second London,' I supply. He is momentarily irritated.

'Yes, yes. You are asking, I am telling, and now I am emphasising.'

I asked him if he ever made tea in his little guards van. He laughed again.

'This is not the place for making tea. This is the guards van.'

It was small and neat and bare. Everything was just as it should be according to regulations laid down, and when he stepped from it for the last time, there would be nothing to say that he, Abdullah, had ever been there in the first place. By then, he would have worked the same line for thirty-eight years. It was his plan to help his son start a nursing home; thereafter, to enjoy the fruits of his pension.

The rain, while it lasted, did lend Bangalore something of London. Murray's *Handbook* identified Spencer's as the best hotel in town: it is still there, but as an annexe to the greater glory of the West End Hotel, which has swallowed it. The West End has handsome flowers, a swimming pool, and a teleprinter. Its grass is green, and during the racing season it is crowded. More accommodation is being added; this was the case in every hotel I stayed at in India. And the bulk of the labouring is done by women and girls.

Gandhi dubbed the untouchable castes Harijans – the Children of God. His attempt to raise caste as an issue of Indian politics has succeeded to the point where, on the statute book, there is no caste: but of course, it exists, and the attitudes underlying it remain. European visitors tend to see Harijans at the moment when they, the tourists, are at their most susceptible. In Bombay I watched women carry away the spoil from a huge hole in the ground. By night, the hole flooded. In the morning the women carried little steel pans of slurry up a steep ramp, gallon by gallon, hour after hour, until the hole was empty. Men whose job it was to dig the hole deeper, who had been watching and waiting impassively, then leaped into the diggings and squabbled about the right and wrong way to do the job. At the top of a ramp was a foreman or overseer, who sat on a stool with a drawing on his knee. A little further back from him, a supervisor of foremen in a suit. The lower bosses arrived by bicycle, the greater by car; and so on. Once, medieval Europe was just so; but perhaps it is only in India where the special cruelty of caste operates so fiercely against the lowest. The lowest in India do seem almost beneath human consideration.

They were rebuilding in the West End at Bangalore. The structure was a two-storey concrete frame. A pulley-hoist was being operated by two young girls. They would fill the basket to the brim, take up the slack on the rope, and then run down a short slope, dragging the load up the side of the building. At the top, it would sway there while the men chatted and called to each other. They, the girls, would be leaning into the rope, every muscle of their backs and legs quivering. Swimmers going to their rooms to change, or those walking to the terrace for an iced drink had to duck under the taut rope. I never saw anyone so much as glance at these girls: nor did anyone on the roof throw them a word. They were simply the lowest of natures. They were Harijans.

From Bangalore to Mysore it is a relatively short hike of three hours. The train runs west now, through a more green and rounded countryside. I travelled second class for some of the way. The carriages are open plan, and have wooden benches. In the first-class accommodation the traveller submits to the longueurs of the journey by sleeping – and so he does here, too, except that every inch of space is taken up. The seats, the luggage racks, the corridors and all the floor space are filled with patient forms. That patience doesn't seem like resignation, but nor does it seem benign. There is little conversation. When I struck up a friendship with my neighbour, every eye was on us, watching intently.

He was an actor, travelling with his wife and three children. The previous night, he had played with one of the great filmstars of Madras, and now he was going home to wait for more work.

'I am all sorts of actor – classical, mythological, social.'

'Do you like an actor's life?'

He considered the question warily.

'Yes,' he said, at last. 'Now it is a good life. I have satisfaction in the art.'

Although very few people could understand us, no one asked him what he was saying. We sat back smiling at each other.

He represents an interesting side to things, that actor. There are very few forms of social enquiry in India, and certainly neither the films nor the stage is one of them. The cinema is enjoying a terrific boom, along the lines of America in the thirties, but the product of the studios is pure escapism. The day I met the actor, there had been a curious report in the paper. Sobha, one of the rising young stars, had committed suicide. On hearing this, one of her distraught fans had gone out, bought a sari of the style she always wore and hanged himself in it. He was described by his parents as a quiet young man without fault, whose only passion had been going to the cinema twice a day. He had ready opportunity. In Cochin, at the end of my journey, I counted forty-two picture houses showing thirty-seven separate titles. (By their own description, many of these films are twaddle, although occasionally a billing will seem to tweak a sensitive nerve: *The Perfect Story!! Conflict between love and emotions!* And following me around like an albatross was the newest disaster movie, a tale of derring-do called *The Burning Train.*)

I met a Madras film unit a little further south. The director and script-writer were good-humouredly setting up the afternoon's shoot. The location was a grove of eucalyptus overlooking a lake, and the cast were cooking lunch. There were a great many of them – dancing girls, an orchestra, a dozen stuntmen, and the principals. All those who appeared in front of the camera wore outrageous pan make-up. I asked the director what the film was about.

'Well you see we are actually shooting four films at once here. This morning we had a wedding scene. Very nice. Plenty of music. This afternoon we are doing a rape. And some stunts.'

He was an elderly man, in the style of John Huston, and regretted the necessity of story-lines that centred round rape. But the theme is becoming more and more dominant. At first sight it might seem that this *is* a case of cinema responding to social concerns, for there is a growing lobby in the cities to have rape and sexual violence brought out into the open. The commonest victims are of course unfortunate Harijans, and the papers were full of a notorious case brought against two police officers. But the film treatment of the harrowing of women in India is not profound, and hardly even significant. It is on a par with drawing attention to broken necks by publicising high-wire acts. In this film, the rape was attended by motor-cycle stunts. A young boy held out an X-ray plate.

'What is this?'

'It is the fingers broken in my hand.'

'You've cut your lip open, too.'

'Yes, I was escaping from the scene, and had to jump the bike into that hollow.'

He pointed to a huge crater in the earth.

'Did you get rehearsal time?'

He laughed and shook his head.

'Did you work out how to do it?'

'I just did it. There is only one way to do it. You can see.'

I had gone out to the location by cab, at the suggestion of the driver, who knew all about films, having appeared in them himself (and in that sense India is like California, at least as far as cab drivers go). He measured the leap the boy had taken and shook his head.

'He's not very good,' he whispered.

'Could you do it?'

'Of course. A *big* crash.' He pointed to a huge man-mountain. 'This is very good stuntman. He is in many films, much money.'

The men involved in the film stood at the foot of the hill, chaffing the boy with the broken hand. Up at the top, the dancing girls sat huddled under the shade of a bush, their eyes averted. They did not speak to each other, nor did they speak to anyone else. They were comprehensively ignored. In that morning's paper were reports of fifty people drowning in a pleasure boat excursion. Another fifty had been burned to death elsewhere. In Murzapur, villagers were experiencing the worst drought in living memory. Three-quarters of the population were completely without water and had dug down 200 feet through solid rock in their despair. The dancing girls fluttered like parakeets. Grips were manhandling huge reflectors into position ready for the afternoon shoot. The director ate ruminatively from food cooked for him on the spot over open fires.

It was part of the journey, this sense of helpless indignation I felt at the location in the eucalyptus trees. India can be enraging: so is it in America sometimes; so can any place be. It isn't very creditable, this exasperation, but it is human. What makes it all the more so is the urge to report the other side of the coin – the beauty and simplicity of things, the natural elegance and grace of people, the coaxing magic of new horizons. But a country isn't all sunsets, and in India particularly, you are as much teased by what is there under your nose as what is promised over the next hill; or tomorrow.

On the way to Mysore, the train runs over the sacred Cauvery river, a great boulder-strewn current of pale green water, attended on its banks by

hundreds of women washing. In the centre of the stream is an island with
the ruins of bath-houses by its shore, and two pagoda-shaped temples. The
place is called Srinangapatnam and once was the residence of a Viceroy of
the Vijayanagar Kingdom, which in its day was considered to be the
highest civilisation that man could raise anywhere. It was utterly swept
away in the course of a few months by an alliance of Muslim Princes. The
capital city of Vijayanagar was twenty-four miles round, and within its
walls were mighty temples and palaces of marble. These, and all the
dwellings, were abandoned, and began the reversionary life of all
civilisations in India, back to dust and weeds. On Srinangapatnam there
remained only the two temples. It was here that Tipu Sultan made his last
stand against the British in 1799.

Tipu was one of those figures who sent a thrill of horror through the
London coffee-houses in the days when the by-word for Indian princes and
their politics was deviousness. In the present-day guides he is pictured in
heroic terms, but it is an unconvincing portrait. With French help, he
fortified the river-island with massive walls, and hid behind them, in hopes
of Napoleon's invasion of Egypt. In his dungeons were chained up a few
officers of the British unwise enough to have been captured. At his court,
all the talk was of turning back the clock, making a new military alliance
with the shattered power of the French in India, and flinging out the
redcoats.

The British marched from Madras and very uncharacteristically
attacked across the fast-flowing Cauvery at 1.30 in the afternoon, in the
very hottest season of the year. Among their party was the Earl of
Mornington's brother, young Arthur Wellesley, destined within a few
years to be created Duke of Wellington for his exploits in another, nearer-
to-home peninsula. The contemporary prints show Highlanders in kilts
and bonnets plunging recklessly into the glassy-green river: the wall was
breached and almost immediately Tipu was killed. He had his palace at the
southern end of the narrow island. All its treasure was carried off, and the
place flattened to the ground. The roofbeams were pulled down, and they
turned up again in some unlikely places. In the ruins of a hut, the victors
found a four-year-old boy, and him they raised up as the Hindu Rajah of
Mysore. The French observers fled, and the last guttering of any other
European interest in India was extinguished. In this one brief action, the
British had secured the whole of south India, coast to coast.

Mysore's history was closely tied up with that of Srinangapatnam. In

the days of the Vijayanagar Kingdom, the chiefs of Mysore paid its
viceroy tribute there. Then, when it fell, Mysore rose. And then there
came Tipu, who destroyed the centre of Mysore city and tried to build
another in its place, called Mazarabad. When he fell, the stones of
Mazarabad were carried back to Mysore, and the young Rajah was set up
on a throne found in a lumber room. But the place found its true eminence
after 1888, when Mysore was created a Native State. Then the magnificence of the Rajahs found expression in their palaces. In the very centre of
the city are the great palace and gardens of the Raj, which are lit every
Sunday by electric light bulbs, thousands of them, picking out the
principal building like a Blackpool illumination. The descendants of all
those ancient quarrels mill about in their thousands in the grounds. For
the single hour during which this takes place, it is said to cost the
municipal authorities 3000 r. (£1666) to give them this pleasure. For the
delectation of his more honoured guests, the Rajah built the Lalitha Mahal,
a summer place on the south-eastern edge of the city, nestling under the
sacred hill of Chamundi.

It is now, quite unbelievably, a hotel. It is not, in popularity, one of the
great hotels of India, although it deserves to be. I booked in there at £10 a
night and had the run of it – a massive late Victorian and Edwardian piece
of elegance. It was explained that Indira Gandhi is wont to stay in the
suite I occupied, which is called, to suit the occasion, the Viceroy Suite or
the Honeymoon Suite. There were altogether four rooms containing three
double beds in that suite, and it is hard to say whether that is the expected
accommodation of viceroys or honeymooners. On the ground floor, the
marble corridors are filled with club armchairs upholstered in red velvet,
and the dining room shimmers with crystal. It is the cliché of Indian royal
magnificence, the Lalitha Mahal.

At sunset, you look out from its handsome balconies over the smoky
plain, back into the city, where the music of flutes seems to rise out of the
ground. On your left is the isolated peak of Chamundi, with a temple at the
top. Up until the time of Tipu's father, they threw people from the highest
cliff to appease the gods. Halfway down is the huge Bull of Nandi, cut from
a single massive rock, polished with oil, and attended by Shivite priests.
And there you are, playing at princes. There were only two small
shortcomings to my stay: the hotel staff were on strike, and I was
convinced I was going to die of fever.

The strike was a very Indian affair. It was unofficial to the point of being completely undeclared. It simply happened that nothing worked, and orders for meals, or a drink, were collected with suave attention, but never acted upon. The waiters simply disappeared. The busiest activity in the hotel was from monkeys, who wandered about the premises without fear. Once a day, parties of sightseers who were under the impression that the Palace was a museum came into the Viceroy Suite and studied me – and the monkeys – for a while before leaving, muttering. It was all very surreal.

But all this was as nothing to the fever I contracted. There never was anything very intrepid about my journey, but Mysore was the lowest and most abject point of it. The last clear memory I had for three days was watching the sun go down while musing on the vagaries of history. Thereafter, history and everything else went out of the window. I slept and sweated on the three beds of the Viceroy suite in turn, reeling off them only to crawl to the bathroom and plunge into a cold bath, gibbering with self-pity and composing wild cables home. Images whirled: Mysore at sunset, when the air is madder and the streets a steely blue, the figures in them the colour of milk; a crazed youth in a main street in Bangalore, completely naked and grey with dust, hurling rocks at cars; the green composure of a station like Yelahanka; pieces of quartz and cornelian out on the Deccan too hot to pick up; the huge and trusting eyes of children begging. I came out of the fever lighter by pounds, and in the wreckage of Mrs Gandhi's home-from-home in Southern India. It was very much like being paid back for impudence. A country, after all, is not just its politics or its history, nor come to that its leaders. As if to make the point, the monkeys very disobligingly stole my pipe and tobacco. As I left, waiters were standing around watching workmen clearing up the damage from a storm. Some at least of the thunder and lightning in my head had also been for real.

'In this weather, we see the cobras coming into the hotel,' the bar steward observed laconically.

To the south of Mysore are the hills of the Nilgiris, the 'Blue Mountains'. You cannot go by rail, but must make the ascent by cab or bus through two game-parks, along ninety miles of road that grows more and more steep. I was heading for Ootacamund, lovingly abbreviated to Ooty by generations of British. The Nilgiris were the last refuge of the aboriginal tribes of South India. At their highest point they are over 8500 feet above sea-level. The Todas, who fled to these mountains away from the endless politics of India, believed the highest peaks to be inhabited by the keeper of the gates of

Heaven: it is very wild country still, except for the astonishing town of Ooty itself.

Ooty was created from nothing to be the hill-station of south India. Explored at the turn of the nineteenth century, it was settled, largely by enterprising Scots, in the 1830s, and designed as a summer residence for the governor of Madras. The Church of St Stephen's was built from those roofbeams, torn from Tipu's palace over ninety miles away, and they stand as emblem of all that Ooty has to offer. For every single thing that now exists on this delectable mountaintop was carried up by dogged and enterprising idealists. The trees, the plants, the flowers, the buildings, the recreations and amusements – everything. From the dense jungle, the British carved out a little idyll, and then filled it with ideas and material objects that had never before been seen there. They planted tea and coffee; they opened out gardens, and made boating lakes. They took to racing, golf, and fishing for trout. The game of snooker was given its rules here. (In 1875, Colonel Sir Neville Chamberlain augmented the game of Black Pool at his station in Jubbalore. A few years later, he was staff officer at Madras, and on one of his summer visits to Ooty, he posted the rules of the game in the Ooty Club. This was attested to in 1938 by two major-generals and a field-marshal, former colleagues and playing partners of Chamberlain, in letters to the *Billiard Player*.)

Ooty started to lose its British population after Independence. The last permanent resident of the Club was the delightful veteran, Colonel Willis, with whom I played a very one-sided memorial match in the snooker room. He is the last of 150 years of British occupation of Ooty, and very fittingly a soldier. There is in Ooty an unmistakable tone of army life, for all that it is a civilian town. Wellington, the garrison town, is nine miles away. But the mood of Ooty is still the jocular yet severe good humour of the officer-caste. The little bungalows seem to echo pleasant remembrances of Sussex, Wiltshire or Dorset. The gardens are full of flowers, and the lawns are mown to perfection. I recovered from Mysore Madness in a garden house of the Savoy Hotel called Iris Cottage. In the evening there was table tennis under the eaves of the verandah; and by day, elegant Indian ladies sat in a swing seat while their tea cooled in a white china service.

Yet in the centre of the town that strange restless sifting of India is already taking place. At Charing Cross, with its roundabout sporting a fountain decorated with hideous little plaster cherubim, there is the present-day addition of a Russian book agency, carrying texts from the

Soviet Union. The enterprising Chinese who followed the wealth up the
mountain peer out from doors overlooking a more dour main street than
will be remembered by the British who once thronged it. The travel agent
has a poster, not of London, but of Singapore. In the shoe shop, a smart
little girl wobbles about on platform soles that threaten to pitch her on her
face: her mother watches in Italian jeans and a stunning white silk blouse.
Outside, a crazed beggar crawls on her hands and knees, screaming for
alms. Ponies run loose in the street, interrupting the blessing of a new taxi
by a garlanded crowd. From being a hill-station, Ooty is fast reverting to a
town on top of a mountain.

For over fifty years it was serviced by a road and tonga-cart track from
its southern side, but for the whole of this century, the pride and joy of
Ooty has been its own hill-railway, the spectacular Nilgiris Express. The
first company to attempt a railway up the mountain went bankrupt, and
you can quite see why. At its steepest, the gradient is one in twelve, and the
line has some dizzying features. For example, you may emerge from a
tunnel directly on to a soaring bridge, or look forward from a station only
to see the tracks apparently disappear over a precipice fifty yards ahead.
For the steepest part of the descent, the engine engages racks set in the
middle of the track, and is hauled down, the locomotive at the front. The
engines are four-cylinder compounds to cope with the rails and the rack,
and there are four independent sets of brakes. It helps to take these little
reassurances to heart because the journey itself is one of the most
spectacular in India. By their efforts, the British transformed the top of the
mountain into parkland, but beyond Coonor, where the rack and pinion is
engaged, you are taken through some of the most hair-raising mountain
scenery imaginable. As you go, the temperature and humidity increase,
until at Mettupallayam you are returned to the steamy heat of palm
plantations. Looking back, you see the mountains that hide Ooty swagged
with cloud like the flounces to a Victorian piano.

Mysore and Ooty go together in my recollection of India. I was abjectly
ill in one place, and comically convalescent in the other. Quite by chance, I
made of Ooty what it was always intended to offer – a place to recuperate in
as benign a climate as you can find anywhere. I fished, I even played golf. I
listened to the World Service on valve radio, lit fires in Iris Cottage by
evening and sipped a drink much recommended by my snooker partner, gin
and ginger beer. I even held bemused conversations with England.

'. . . pulled the guttering down over the front door.'

'What? Who pulled the guttering down?'

'The *snow*.'

'Ah yes,' (defensively) 'well, I have been very ill.'

'Very well?'

'*No*. Very ill.'

The journey down the mountain was a necessary one, for a few more days and I think I would have succumbed to the charm of the place. Because it is so artificial, Ooty is doubly seductive: I, who had set my face against the British Raj, now began to feel nobbled by it. Mettupallayam, at the foot of the mountain, was an instant medicine for that sort of thing.

The normal route is to get to the broad-gauge station of Coimbattur, and very few travellers stop off at Mettupallayam. I had booked a seat on the Teagarden Express, but was set upon in the station by a garrulous booking clerk.

'I am waiting to go home to my missus to see you. You have perhaps brought me something from the excellent Savoy Hotel?'

'Um, what, exactly?'

'Oh, some plum pudding or something of the sort.'

I looked back up the mountain doubtfully. Had I missed anything? The clerk applied a little more pressure.

'Perhaps some pens, or some coins from England? This trouser you are wearing, this is very fine. How many suitings have you in your luggage?'

'None.'

He laughed disbelievingly.

'You can tell me. Three, four?'

'I don't own a suit.'

'Well, well,' he sighed. 'And you have no plum pudding?'

A traveller pulled me to one side.

'Do not give this man anything,' he whispered.

'That's easy enough. He keeps asking for plum pudding.'

My confidant raised a warning finger. He hissed noisily in my ear: 'Do not give it to him, sir. On any account.'

Instead, I walked out into the town. It was the hour before sunset, and the sky an amazing mauve, slashed by orange clouds. The sun hung in the horizon like a huge ball. Mettupallayam is a return to India with a vengeance, for it is a town without European history. Once, in the 1890s, the railway arrived here from Madras and they set about climbing the Ghat to Ooty, but none of that elegance and composure still to be found at the top of the mountain has touched in any way the town at the bottom. It is, and perhaps always will be, a glorified trading-post. It was like coming back to earth with a bump, walking down the long main street, and the niceties of hill-station life suddenly seemed massive irrelevancies. The glances were frank, and not specially warm. I stopped for coffee, standing out in the street while the man poured the scalding stuff from one steel cup to another, with a sardonic flourish, the better to cool it.

Mettupallayam is a town only because I describe it so, as it has a population of a handy size. I saw no public buildings, and the place has next to no public amenities. The most modern shop was a beaten-up record bar, which displayed some unusual and coveted jazz items. The sleeves were empty. Had there ever been the records that went with these covers? The proprietor, a young man, shrugged carelessly. If he knew, he was not saying.

What there is in Mettupallayam, of course, is people, clustering together as if afraid of the empty places and driving each other in poverty and wretchedness, for the benefit of a very few richer men. It is a community without, apparently, a middle class. There, you are poor, or you are rich, and the possession of anything – a bicycle, a sewing machine, an ox, a bag of metalworking tools – is wealth. In the foothills of the Nilgiris, along the road that pre-existed the railway, is a boy of about twenty. He sits by a little freshet of water that bursts from the rock, and in his hands is a rusty litre can. He will sell you his water to top up your radiator. He charges a rupee and is a rich man. A mile or so above him, at a particular bend in the road, is an old woman. Every so often a lorry dumps a block of stone about the size of an easy chair on her patch of ground, and she chips away at it with a stone wrapped in a wet cloth. I asked if she were dressing the boulder for building purposes. My guide was a good-looking taxi-driver. He took the question to be a joke against the old woman, and then when I did not laugh, looked perplexed. What she was doing was more basic. She was making ballast for the railway. When she had reduced the huge boulder to chips, a lorry arrived and left her the next one. This woman is poor.

Riches and poverty, explained at this level, humble even the most confident traveller. Up on the mountain, the people of Ooty had, for 150 years at any rate, the fabrication of a social order that was not without its cruelty, but was at any rate clear and concise. It is interesting that to make things work, the very landscape itself, down to the least plant and flower, was changed. Mettupallayam is, by comparison, the truer witness. That night, as the sun fell, the streets were teeming with business and the industry that comes from a broad back or a strong pair of legs. People streamed past me while I drank my coffee – young girls with huge bundles of wattle on their heads, men manhandling sacks, all of them sucking hungrily at the moist air. Far away is the State capital. Further, among a people few of them have ever seen, the Central Government. Do they really belong to the same nation, or share the aspirations of the leader? They live in a halfway house, between fieldwork and the benefits of community: if they read the city papers, do they experience the same bewilderment as I did? Like everyone else on this earth, they did not choose their parents, nor their place of birth. What did they make of me, 5000 miles from home, a traveller from a country adjusting to being poor, yet, for all that, rich and purposeful beyond their dreams?

Something happened there in Mettupallayam. I suppose there is a moment in every traveller's tale that can't be rendered quite as glibly as the moon over the temple, or the soughing of palms. What happened, without making too much of a mystery of it, was more the stuff of fiction. That is to say, I could convey it by fiction and in no other way. To be sure, there was a charge in the air, an atmospheric. As night fell, the clouds about the mountain grew dark and bruised, and the most startling mauve light began to appear in the street, sweeping away the detail of the place. Lamps were lit, and the record shop played distorted pop songs. Now the people passing were dark shadows, or sudden illuminations of red cloth and brown flesh. The whole place seemed to be saying to me: *write this*. Except, of course, things like this are not written until a long time after. There is a point at which the eye ceases to see.

I walked back to the station. The troublesome clerk had gone. I could see his quarters, which he had pointed out to me, lit by a single lamp, and while I gazed, the first spats of rain began to fall. Within a minute or so, the skies opened, and within another few minutes, the power on the station failed. The Teagarden Express was shunted in through an utter darkness, unlit. We boarded, and for an hour or more the carriages remained without light. The man who had spoken to me earlier shuffled conspiratorially out of the gloom.

'Tonight,' he hissed, 'you must lock the door. It is better.'

With which, he locked himself and his family in with a crash of bolts. At last some wan light came on in the train, and I read for a little while. And what I read was this, from Kafka: 'Because of impatience, we were driven out of Eden, and because of impatience, we can never return.'

The train stirred uneasily, and we gently pulled away for Cochin, the destination I had picked with such lightheartedness in Bombay.

I stayed awake until the small hours on that last journey. We hauled through the night, from time to time stopping at unknowable halts where perhaps a twink of white gleamed for a moment as someone in a shirt skipped to the embankment and then dropped down again. Or perhaps the train would crawl past some huts, the interiors lit by wobbling dishes of light, and peopled by shadows. Every so often we came to a station, with hundreds sleeping and scores more moving around or coming to stare through the open windows of the train with impassive curiosity.

At dawn on that last morning, I hung out of the doors gazing out on a landscape that sprang almost from fantasy. In the powdery first light that seemed to drift and cling as fine as talc, the outlines of great palms established themselves. We rumbled across bridges and over lagoons, and huffed our way through villages of palm-frond huts. Some of the most beautiful people in the world were rising, lithe and brown, wrapping their bodies in cotton shifts, or stretching at doorways. There was a sunrise booming out of water stretched as thin as silver foil. Kerala, the last of the four states I had travelled through, was waiting to greet me. We pulled into Cochin Harbour Terminus while the sky was still a delicate rose, the smoke from the locomotive flying like a banner.

A journey has not one but many destinations. Cochin provided a rich variety of them. From the Harbour Terminus, you can look out on ships loading with spices, and back on a workaday railway yard that has none of the glamour of a big-city station. The line ends, unromantically, in a set of buffers and a poor sort of station without frills. But in what is called Fort Cochin, you can see the church in which Vasco da Gama was buried or read the inscriptions on headstones erected by the Dutch. St Francis Xavier preached on these shores, and it was in Cochin that the Jesuits published the first book ever printed in India. The Portuguese, the Dutch, the Danes, the English traded here. There is a community of Jews founded in the fifth century, and at about the same time the first of the Nazarani, disciples of St Thomas, landed. Syrian Catholics mingle with the Hindu aristocracy of Cochin, the Nairs.

The very landscape sows confusion. For someone only newly accustomed to the heat and dust of the plains, or fresh from the pleasant artifice of the hill-station, Cochin is a baffling place. It is a peninsula that is, by the complexity of its channels and inlets, as good as an island. The train track ends at Willingdon Island, which is entirely artificial and the result of dredging in the deep-water channel. On Willingdon, the bars are full of captains waiting for a cargo. And yet across the water in Fort Cochin and Mattancherri there is a more ancient past. Every traveller who has been to Cochin has visited Jews Town, or the Chinese fishing nets, or the Dutch Palace. It is what a tourist comes to see, after all, and Cochin answers cheerfully to two tourist titles–Queen of the Arabian Sea, and the Venice of the East. But tourism is a reduction of travel in the same way travel is a reduction of domicile. At night, you can see special performances of Kathakali dancing. By day, you can stand in the street and be dazzled by the sun reflected in the glass of a hundred pictures of the Christian saints, and look past that shop to a hammer and sickle flying from a bamboo pole. You can find a cathedral with a cross rooted in a lotus, glance to your left and see a call for all-out strike. What you can't do, in this welter of conflicting evidence, is render it words. One realisation that I had arrived at an emphatic destination was when I found I needed to write nothing in my journal.

It is a green and watery place, Cochin, and as unlike the received idea of India as it is possible to be, but it really was the perfect place to finish. The people are beautiful and the complexity of the scenery such that every hundred yards is a new discovery and another delight. In an exalted mood, I crossed a channel by ferry to a village called Cumbalenghe. The houses on either side of the street were given over to the making of coir ropes, and on the beach a marching band was playing. The costumes were military and the tune from a recent movie. But somehow or other the moment was a perfect expression of the pleasures of travel, the strange unguessable endings the best journeys always have. Perhaps to an Indian, most probably to a Western student of India, it wasn't India, those last few paces of my journey. But I was rapt. Until my journey from Bombay to Cochin, I had always considered rail-travel as no more than a narrow corridor in time, a passage of hours and nothing else. Going by train in that wide crescent cured me of that idea for ever. The next day, walking out on to the tarmac to board my airbus, I blessed the trains that had brought me there. Without the journey there can be no destination, and to have the mystery at Cumbalenghe, with its exquisite sadness, was only possible because of the awakened heart that going by train had wrought.

SOUTH AFRICA

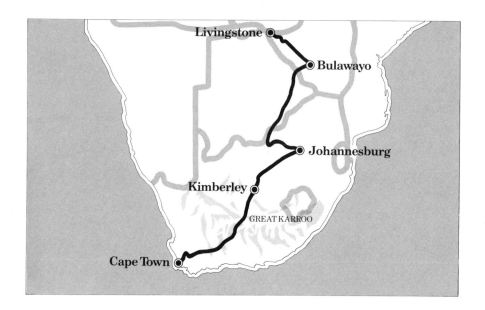

Zambezi Express

MICHAEL WOOD

In the autumn of 1979 I went to southern Africa in the privileged position of a journalist and traveller. I was to retrace Cecil Rhodes' railway route from Cape Town to Victoria Falls, from the mother city of the whites in Africa to Lobengula's indaba tree. The railway had been Rhodes' dream, part of a strip of British Empire red right up Africa. He it was who financed the push to the Zambezi in the 1890s, where (having disposed of Lobengula, king of the Matabele) he founded a country and named it after himself: Rhodesia. My journey, then, was his: into the heart of Africa.

And what a time to do it! That November Rhodesia was teetering on the edge. Fifteen years after a UDI which was intended to inaugurate 1000 years of white supremacy, the illegal and racialist regime of Ian Smith had very rapidly come face to face with History. For eight years now the black nationalists of the Patriotic Front had been fighting a full-scale guerilla war against the white settlers to win back the land seized by Rhodes in the 1890s. Declaring themselves Lobengula's heirs by proxy, they consulted the spirit mediums of the people; they swore their oaths on the dead freedom fighters of the failed revolt of 1897; they had even determined that their new country would bear the name Zimbabwe, after the great stone city which is the supreme architectural achievement of the ancient black races of Rhodesia (an achievement which hard-line whites denied them). Now, despite heavy losses, the Patriotic Front controlled much of the countryside. And now, around the conference table at Lancaster House in London, they were negotiating with the British government and the Smith regime to obtain a free election.

The war had already displaced hundreds of thousands of people into protected villages and the black townships around Salisbury. A quarter of a million more had fled to refugee camps in Botswana, Zambia and Mozambique, where they were living in destitution. A million head of cattle had been lost. There was devastation, disease and malnutrition. When I set off on 16 November from Cape Town, the war was still being fought while the PF talked. It might be over by the time I reached the Falls. If it ended, where would that leave South Africa, Rhodesia's chief ally, and their illegally held colony in Namibia, where another guerilla war was increasing in severity? And if talks broke down, would war eventually engulf the whole of southern Africa, drawing in all Rhodesia's neighbours? Such thoughts gave me a sharp sense of anticipation at the start of the journey. Whatever happened, the next weeks would be unrepeatable.

Cape Town 16 November 1979. 'You must take the Blue Train,' everyone said, 'it's the most luxurious train in the world.' That had never struck me as a reason to travel. Quite the reverse, in fact: I always seem to have chosen the most eccentric and decrepit ways of getting to places. But South Africa is a land of the most violent contrasts, and somehow with its vaunted luxury the Blue Train seemed an appropriate way to begin this venture into the interior.

Twice a week the Blue Train runs the thousand miles from the Cape to Pretoria. In the old days it used to meet the Union Castle liners, and it pre- serves that vanished air of pre-war gentility. It is a diesel train with absolute self-confidence. It ignores the outside world. At a sedate forty miles an hour it transports its pampered passengers smoothly and soundlessly behind windows tinted with pure gold to keep down the glare. There is a private suite with lounge and bathroom; a bar in whose leafy corner one might see a

The Blue Train

bridge class in progress; a pince-nez *maître d'hôtel* whose fastidious regard would do credit to Claridges. This, in short, is a train on which travel itself is the destination.

The first hours of the journey pass through the fertile, temperate plains of Cape Province with their vineyards and oak trees in the lee of the grandiose spurs and fairytale peaks of the Drakenstein. This was the heartland of the original Dutch settlers of the seventeenth century, who built their farms in the delectable valleys around Paarl and Stellenbosch. Their descendants – Afrikaners, Africans, as they call themselves – have formed the ruling élite in South Africa since 1948. It was they who regularised forms of racial separation already practised in British colonies south of the Zambezi into apartheid, the total separation of black and white races. Of course they are now a state under siege. If not yet physically, then certainly spiritually.

You would not know it from the wealth and self-confidence of the Blue Train's clientèle. To them events beyond the Limpopo are a mote in the mind's eye. But at the lunch table Willem de Clerc, a tenth-generation

Afrikaner who farms near Paarl, shook his head sadly: 'We are not a strange people, we are a very human people, but they thought they could change the world. This is a reformed society. Like the English revolution, or the communists, or the Jacobins in France, they thought a political system could provide all the answers in human life. It's like Hamlet – you know how that ends – the bodies piling up around him.'

A state under siege. At Paarl there are three massive, pale-coloured granite boulders, like debris from some planetary ice age. The largest is a mile in circumference. A mile! It was named Paarl, 'pearl', in 1657 by an early Dutch settler who thought it glistened like a pearl in the sunshine after rain. On the top, reaching far into the blue sky, is the Taalmonument, the Language Monument. 'It symbolises the origin and development of our language here over the three hundred years,' said my lady companion in the cocktail bar. 'We say that Afrikaans is "*n Perel van Groot Waarde*", a pearl of great worth', she added. In what other country could you find a monument to a language erected by the people who speak it? You might expect it to have been erected in the heroic days of the nineteenth-century struggles with the British, or maybe in 1948. But no. It was built in 1975. When you become hated by most of your fellow citizens in the world, you have to define very clearly what it is you are fighting for.

The route which the train now follows is the route by which the whites penetrated into the interior, first by ox carts through a precipitous and almost trackless mountain terrain, on the trail of the transhumant Bantu; later by the railway tracks which were laid up the Hex River in the late 1870s and early 80s, rising from the orchards of Worcester (750 feet above sea level) to the top of the pass at nearly 3600 feet, higher than the summit of Table Mountain.

The Blue Train climbs the Hex River Pass by an extraordinary series of curves, some only 100 yards in diameter, so that at one point the front and rear of the train are parallel to each other, going in opposite directions! At the top there is a spectacular view of the 7000-foot peak of the Matroosberg on the one hand, and stretching back below us the rich vineyards of the Hex valley. Then, within a couple of hours, there is a dramatic change in the landscape. We enter a wilderness like nowhere else on earth. The Great Karroo, the Hottentot 'Land of Thirst'.

Into this 'worn-out emaciated land without soil or verdure' (as a nineteenth-century traveller put it) the Afrikaners made their Great Trek in the 1830s, away from the British overlords of the Cape to find a new promised land. They called it New Eden: a land of baked wastes broken by sills of ancient rock and protruding kopjes blazing hot by day and cold, black, starry brilliant by night. Here hardy farmers of Dutch and British stock still make their living from this intransigent soil, scratching fertile oases in an immensity of scrub. Treeless, dun-coloured and crumbling, the soil of the Karroo comes alive only infrequently when the rain makes gullies run with water and a carpet of red and blue flowers springs overnight, as from nowhere. But in some places in the Karroo there has been no rain now for three years.

Life cannot be viewed through gold windows. At five o'clock the Blue Train stopped at Touws River to change engines. I decided to get off there, to see something of the people who live by the track. From the conditioned air of the Blue Train I stepped on to the platform and into a sunlight that falls like a heavy weight on the head and shoulders; the eyes narrow with the glare; the air is dry and hot and smells of the surrounding mountains, of gorse and (is it?) thyme. No one else gets off. The Blue Train's doors hiss shut, and soon its last coach disappears in the heat haze in front of the red hills towards Lainsburg.

The familiar images of the Karroo: the wind pump, the white farmhouse with its cluster of pepper trees out of sight of its neighbours' chimney smoke. A perpetual frontier country; a drought-stricken land where the landlords make their money from sheep or nothing. The Afrikaners are fond of saying that their oldest tradition is their feel for the land, and out here everything has a biblical simplicity: the throat-cutting of the sheep for the owner's monthly gift to the workers; the weekly hand-outs of water, meal, coffee and sugar; the poverty of the workers themselves, most of them itinerant, earning thirty or forty Rand a month; their stoical resignation.

'We hope the Lord will help us so that life gets better than it is now,' Maria said to me, sturdy wife of a deaf mute farm hand, 'then I might like the Karroo. As it is, we have to work in the Karroo because only some bosses understand my husband: it's the bosses here who know him. I've no choice. I've three children still at school. I must stay here now. He's my legal husband. If I'd been alone I would have gone somewhere else. It may be better for my children. White people we've worked for say I bring them up well. My daughter wants to be a welfare worker. The boy wants to be a carpenter. The baby – he's nine – says he will work on the railways. They earn good money there.'

Here too is the larger-than-life figure of Oom Dan, the 'old boss', the foreman who rules this farm with a paternal iron rod for the absentee landlord.

'The workers I treat like children, they look on me as their father. I've told them they can call me "meneer", *Mr* Van Vuuren, but they have always called me "baas" and now they want to call me "oubaas". They prefer that. I don't work with them any more, but I go with them wherever they go. Where they work, I sit with them. When they go to the veld they want me with them. Ask them. They'll tell you they haven't got a "radio". They need me because I am their "radio".... As for the life here in the Karroo, I never go to town. Take me to a town, take me away from the farm, and within two months you can bury me.'

Above Dan Van Vuuren's living-room door there is a portrait of D F Malan, the nationalist architect of apartheid. I suppose his compatriots would consider Oom Dan a typical Afrikaner countryman – the man who knows sheep, who knows the veld; a red-necked bull of a man, devout and intolerant, hard as nails; the ruler of his roost. Such were the original Trekkers, one imagines, hard-bitten frontiersmen building their society on traditional Afrikaner virtues – self-sufficiency, a refusal to kow-tow to outside authority, Old Testament fundamentalism and a belief in the divinely ordained supremacy of white over black.

In the next few days I wound my way slowly through the centre of the republic. First from Touws River up to Ladismith on a delightful slow train which starts at two in the morning and can take up to eight hours to do eighty miles. It is an old '24' class built at the Hyde Park Works of the North British Locomotive Company in Glasgow, a smart little branch line engine which chugs slowly up and down this one line twice a week. A pleasant life for a train, I suppose. Its job is to ferry workers to the vineyards of the Ladismith valley, to carry supplies to isolated farms in a region with no made-up roads, and to bring domestic water to tiny, one-horse halts in the long dry season. The locals call the train Makadas. I could not discover why. 'Muck and dust' someone suggested (plausible enough). 'Make a dash' said another (surely not?).

The train was already two hours late by the time dawn came up over Hondewater. But on the Makadas time has no meaning. The traveller must simply sit back on his wooden seat and watch the splendid sunrise touch the far-off tips of the Oudtshoorn range with gold. Then, as the still morning air becomes warmer, listen to the explosive woosh of steam echoing in the crags of the Little Karroo. On this train a local farmer responded memorably to my comments on the efficiency of the service.

'Well, this is an old-fashioned system for sure,' he said, 'but so are we. Diesel is surely not fitting with our mountains. We've just got to have this steam locomotive.' Later on in the journey I would understand his remark.

The Makadas stops at Ladismith. The line was never driven through to Oudtshoorn to join up with the coastal route and the Indian Ocean. The last station on the Oudtshoorn side of the mountains is called Protem, 'so far'. But, in fact, it goes no farther. Ladismith was thus left at the end of the line and nobody goes there today. So, to return to the main line north you must either go back from Ladismith the way you came, or you can cut through the Seven Weeks Pass under 'Magic Mountain' and back by road to Lainsburg.

From Lainsburg it is possible to take any number of trains through the desert northwards. One, the Trans-Karroo Express, is still pulled by steam engines, the 15Fs. Some of these are 'stars', kept in immaculate condition by their crews with whitened wheel rims and cab roofs, coloured number plates, burnished pipes and personal brass emblems: an eagle, a horse, a star. In South Africa the railways are the biggest employers and among the best. Pride in the locomotive is expected and fostered.

At Beaufort West, on the way to De Aar, we are overhauled by a Garratt steaming free at full speed, charging north with no load. 'We are lending several of them to the Rhodesians,' the conductor said in a confidential tone in answer to my question, 'diesels too, and technicians.' A black smudge of smoke hung over the horizon to the north long after the engine had whirled frantically out of sight.

De Aar is not a place you would visit for the fun of it. Central rail junction of the republic, like Crewe and Swindon it is an out-and-out railway colony. It stands in the middle of a hot, howling wilderness, said an early traveller, and it stands there simply because of the railway. Here the main lines go north and south, east and west, carrying minerals, the arterial wealth of South Africa: iron ore, copper, manganese. The distances are terrific: the eight o'clock evening train from De Aar to Windhoek in Namibia, 800 miles away, takes two days. The railyards are all smoke, grime, and coal dust, with hundreds of steam locomotives and thousands of black and coloured workers to service them. These people live in townships which are literally on the other side of the tracks. For them there is a curfew in the white town.

Africans are responsible for the upkeep of the steam engines but are prohibited from driving them

In De Aar it is easy to see why steam has survived in South Africa. The republic has no natural oil deposits of its own. But it does have ample coal. And an almost limitless supply of cheap African labour to maintain the labour-intensive steam locomotives. Cleaning and greasing, but not driving – there are no black drivers in South Africa – white railwaymen do that. 'An old-fashioned system,' said the man on the Makadas. And this is why.

I travelled the next 150 miles to Kimberley on the footplate of one of the giant freight trains going north. The two coupled class 25 giants, *Maria* and *Jennifer*, whose names belie their devastating power, pour columns of black smoke hundreds of feet into the air as they roar at 50 mph past the kopjes of the northern Karroo. Here the landscape is a vivid orange desolation, a place of mirages. This line from De Aar to Kimberley is the steam buff's paradise. Thirty freights a day pull up the long incline to Krankhuil huffing and puffing, shooting unburned coal into the sky. We pass mineral trains going south ('We're pulling it out of Namibia as fast as we can,' someone would later tell me in Kimberley); moving north we saw armaments: for Namibia, Rhodesia, who knows?

We cross the Orange River, the historic dividing line between the original Boer republics and the British imperial possessions in Cape Province. In fact we do not enter the Free State here but skirt its south-western edge, reminding us that the British built this railway to outflank the Boers, via Kimberley through Bechuanaland and on to Rhodesia. While the crew boil their coffee on the end of a rod thrust into the furnace, we pass over the Modder River where the British suffered a humiliating disaster in the Boer War, and then on to Kimberley past a reassuring litany of English and Dutch country stations: Chalk Farm, Heuningneskloof, Spytfontein, Wimbledon – names for an Afrikaner John Betjeman to conjure with.

Kimberley. Those backwoods republics across the Orange and the Vaal rivers might have remained quietly in their inhospitable landscape and never made their mark on history had it not been for the accident of the discovery of mineral wealth: diamonds in Kimberley in 1869, and the subsequent finds of gold on the Witwatersrand in Transvaal in 1887. The conflicts by which the British tried to dominate the Boers and control this wealth – the Boer Wars – have been the determining factors in the politics of South Africa ever since.

Kimberley bears few signs of the rush now. But this was where Rhodes, then Prime Minister of the Cape, made his fortune, signing the biggest cheque ever for the rights to the main mine, the Big Hole. This is what enabled him to finance the construction of a railway 1000 miles to the Zambezi, to found Rhodesia, and to conceive his kingmaking visions of a southern African federation. The Big Hole is his monument. A pit of Babel. It is silent now, filled with water. Like a meteorite crater gouged in the veld, it goes down a thousand feet. 'When I'm in Kimberley,' said Rhodes, 'I often go and sit on the edge of the mine and reckon up the value of the diamonds and the power they conferred. Every foot of that blue ground means so much power.'

History has passed Kimberley by. Rhodes' company, De Beers, still have their head office here, but their operation has moved elsewhere, to the Joburg gold reef and the new diamond mines of Botswana. Kimberley just sits and swelters with its wild west sidewalks, waiting for the one blessing of the African summer, the torrential downpour which comes here punctually every day at five and leaves the awnings streaming, main street aflood with a momentary monsoon.

The go-getters have got up and gone. But behind them is left a strange flotsam. It is a sight you might have seen in the days before the rush – a handful of poor white prospectors, men and women, licensed by De Beers to hand-sieve for loose diamonds in the stony hills above the Vaal river. The temperature is 114 degrees, but men like Lou Bothes still work here as he has for fifty years. An archetypal prospector, Lou lives in the same hut he has had for all that time. At seventy-three he still puts in a full day of back-breaking toil in a claim hole with no corner of shade. He still dreams of finding the big one (and after all, the Cullinan itself was a loose diamond, missed by the diggers).

It is a strange world, the diggers' world. Ruled by dreams, omens and superstitions. It is considered bad luck to have women on a claim; they abandon it altogether if they find a snake in it. Men in white shirts are a good sign, so are dreams of silver fish, of 'dog diamonds' and especially sheep's heads. A diggers' legend here at Noitgedacht has it that the biggest diamond of all will be the shape of a sheep's skull. The sheep's skull drives them on.

'I began this when I was fifteen,' said Lou Bothes. 'I once left and took another job, on the railways, but I soon came back. I'm a digger at heart. The biggest diamond I ever found was fourteen carats. I wanted a thousand pounds for it' (Bothes still counts in the old Cape Colony currency), 'but they would only give me five hundred. I gave the money away: I had my "auntie" to look after, you see!'

'What's so good about this digging life that you stick at it?' I asked. 'I just don't know what it is, man: I've worked myself to death, but I just can't stop this business. I have to go on. I can't go anywhere else now.'

Dawn in the brilliant immensity of the high veld. There is a clarity which was unimaginable to this traveller from the cold north. From a dozen miles away, the plain of Kimberley stretches towards the Kalahari in the palest wash of white sky and white earth, ash of the exhausted volcano in whose heat the diamonds were fused in the blue ground. An immemorial flatness save where the lip of Kimberley kopje marks the site of the ancient convulsions. The place seems extraterrestrial; it creates illusions in the air and in time. At Barkly West, derelict Victorian workings mingle with artefacts from the Stone Age; miners were here before History. Everywhere there are great spoil mounds marked with weathered claim tickets; at Pniel you walk on a river terrace heaped with gravels, tiny gemstones and semi-precious pebbles: agate, jasper, jade. It would be no surprise here, one feels, to stumble on the bleached bones of dinosaurs.

By the middle of the day the temperature was nearly 130 degrees and the mirages were growing more insistent. The polished limestone rocks melted the rubber on my shoes. I fled back to Kimberley with the first signs of heatstroke.

That was a Saturday. The next Monday morning, a week out, I left Kimberley and diverged from the northern route to follow the Blue Train's track into Transvaal. To Johannesburg. Joburg was not on Rhodes' historic railway to the Zambezi – in fact in the 1890s it was hardly a town at all, just shanties – a drinking, whoring, spending, mining camp; the African Klondike. But it is now the political, commercial and racial hub of South Africa, and along with its black satellite towns, it is a magnet to the traveller who wishes to understand what is happening in South Africa today.

You arrive in Joburg past yellow spoil heaps, made from gold workings which go down 11,000 feet below the skyscrapers, so deep as to feel the inner heat of the earth. Joburg is literally and figuratively built on gold. It shows. The place oozes surplus wealth and purchasing power, and has a standard of living unknown elsewhere in Africa. Where else in the western world would you find the lights of skyscrapers blazing top to bottom throughout the night? Here consumption is conspicuous.

Joburg is ringed by black townships which provide the service labour for this wealth. In these townships also live the black migrant gold workers who come from all over southern Africa to the Witwatersrand to make their living, 6000 from Rhodesia, and thousands more from Botswana, Mozambique, Zambia. They live out of sight of white eyes in all-male hostels where violence and death are commonplace.

The biggest of the townships is Soweto. Or rather, So/we/to – South Western Townships – is several rolled into one. It is the home of a million and a half people, and is the largest city in Africa after Cairo. Now the name of Soweto is known throughout the world and has become a rallying call for the oppressed black peoples of South Africa. Here in June 1976, riots which began as a protest about the teaching of Afrikaans in black schools ignited a cry of rage against the treatment of blacks throughout the republic. Soweto, with its urban vitality, aggression and sheer energy, provided the fuse. And of seven hundred killed by the police, four hundred died here. Out of sight of Joburg, on the far side of the buffer zone required by apartheid, Soweto is an hour's journey from Joburg by train; it lies in a

Workers pile into the carriages, or hang on to the outside, as the train takes them to and from work in Johannesburg

shallow bowl of hills which are hung with sulphurous fumes even on a clear summer's day. Soweto is made up of endless lines of identical brick-asbestos bungalows. Miles of them. To go there I needed a special permit, for apartheid works both ways.

Wednesday 5 December. Dube Station, Soweto, soon after dawn. Here too the railways reflect the life of the community. At this ungodly hour while a cold wind whips up the rubbish in the streets, thousands of the people of Soweto are rushing to the trains to take them into Joburg. There are not enough trains, and every one leaves with scores of people hanging on the outsides for dear life, clutching buffers, couplings, window frames, all desperate to get to work. If they are late there are plenty more who will be happy to take their jobs. It is a nightmare scene this, fingers clawing the door frames as the train moves off; crowds of people running across the track; the incessant drone of the loudspeaker drowning all conversation.

I had arranged to meet a journalist friend whom I had met in Joburg, and who covers Soweto affairs for the black edition of the *Star* newspaper.

Derek was standing on the platform looking snappy in a light grey suit. In his voice humour, reason and anger were mixed in equal measure. But humour in particular, which is one of the great qualities of the people of Soweto.

'It's all a question of giving a man his human dignity,' he said, 'his right to vote. They've got to give us that now. I can remember seeing my father bowing and scraping before a white fat cat – "yes boss, no boss, anything you say boss" – cringeing – and it really hurt me as a child to see my daddy who I loved and revered stripped of his dignity as a man. When I grew up I once did that too. But not now. They must give us our rights. You must understand that the people here in Soweto are temporary.'

'What do you mean, temporary?'

'They aren't permanent,' he replied. 'Everyone who works here has to be registered in a homeland where he can be returned. He has to renew the permit each year. You belong to Transkei or Bophuthatswana, not here.'

'Do the people of Soweto feel temporary?' I asked.

'No, they feel quite permanent.' He grinned a wicked grin.

Despite all the 'wind of change' publicity blowing around that autumn, Derek remains unconvinced. He feels that if there have been minor changes in 'social' apartheid, the political structure is as rigid as ever.

That night he took me to Lucky's club in Orlando, Soweto, the only real *club*, as opposed to a shebeen, a drinking house. Lucky is a gentle giant of a man, a man who works hard for his community but who also possesses that Odyssean cunning needed to survive in the jungle of Soweto.

We arrived early, before sunset, and as the light slanted across the billboards at Orlando station, we heard beautiful mellow jazz – Duke Ellington – being played in the room next to Lucky's fish bar. A group of men of all ages was getting it together on battered but cherished instruments. That night we all got drunk and everybody wished to talk about everything – from Charlie Parker to what we British were doing in Northern Ireland, a story even more tortuous than the Afrikaners and the blacks.

Rhodes pushed his railway a thousand miles from Kimberley to the Zambezi in a few years in the 1890s. 'If there be a God,' he said, 'I think he would like me to paint as much of Africa British-Red as possible.' To return to his route from Joburg you must journey west overnight on a standard diesel to a rail town whose name used to appear on every schoolchild's atlas: Mafeking.

I suppose I came here expecting that somehow the Boer War siege would still be tangible. But today another siege is on everybody's lips. And this time there will be no relief for Mafeking. In 1980 the town will be assimilated into the black homeland of Bophuthatswana and henceforth exist only as Mmabatho.

Formerly capital of the British protectorate of Bechuanaland, Mafeking owes its existence to the railways. It is a major junction linking Rhodes' northern route with the gold reef. It was for this reason that the Boers besieged it in the Boer War. Now the railway workshops have gone, Bechuanaland is independent, and if the whites here resist incorporation they will lose all their custom to the neighbouring black 'capital'. 'We'll become a ghost town,' someone said, a *spookdorp*. But in a way that is precisely what Mafeking is, and its real ghosts lie in the cemetery by the railroad track, in a corner of a foreign field that does indeed remain for ever England. For King and Empire it says on the crosses. By the end of that distant war, Kitchener had in South Africa the largest number of British troops ever sent abroad on any expedition. 'We're not forgetting it/we're not regretting it/we're not letting it fade away or gradually die . . .' So they sang in 1901. Now these young men from Lincolnshire and Staffordshire lie forgotten, passed only by the antiquated steam engines in the sidings which shunt up and down all day and pass the weeping willows with a chuff of steam and a mournful whistle.

The fate of Mafeking is the destiny of Mmabatho. To get to Mmabatho you leave Mafeking past the cemetery, then out over drab empty scrub for a mile or two. There the line stretches away to Botswana, Rhodesia, and the copper belts of Zambia and Zaïre. There is nothing else here but thornbushes, and mud-walled huts roofed with corrugated iron sheets weighed down by boulders. Here, the South African government has determined, will be the 'capital' of this new so-called independent homeland. Above the red ant hills, three new buildings have gone up: a block of brown-brick service flats, a stadium of scaffolding, and the crowning glory, the symbol of Bophuthatswanan national prestige, the administrative centre of President Mangope's Bantustan, the Mmabatho Sun Hotel. The architecture is what might be termed Tijuana-Tswana: in front there is an ornamental pool which my caustic friend Frankie insists on calling Lake Mangope within earshot of the chief of police. In the air-

conditioned casino ranks of one-armed bandits are being plied by a crush of
South African whites in short-sleeved shirts. They're 'abroad' here, you see –
there's even a South African Embassy down Lucas Mangope Highway to
prove it. So they can indulge in all the delights forbidden them in the
republic proper, notably gambling, and wining, dining and dancing with
black girls.

The way Derek Thema sees it, the Afrikaners feel that if everyone had
the vote, then that would be the end of a culture which has lasted for over
300 years here. So there must never be a non-white majority. The answer
they have dreamed up is to separate the races territorially and allow the
non-whites to 'develop' with their own culture in their own areas.
Basically then, the idea is that two-thirds of the population get about an
eighth of the land; they have their own government under men like
Mangope, whose decisions can be overruled at any time by Pretoria; they
have no control over arms, right of entry, the presence of South African
police, post offices, roads, railways, harbours, aviation, entry of aliens,
currency, loans, customs and excise. So if the Mmabatho Sun Hotel, this
mini Las Vegas, strikes you as a little bizarre as the 'capital' of a non-
existent state, as a focus for black civil and political aspirations, it plainly
serves to remind us that political aspirations for blacks do not yet exist in
South Africa.

In the Mmabatho Sun Hotel I had to keep pinching myself. But
unbelievable as this white playground is, there is more to come. In the
foyer of the hotel I opened my *Mafeking Mail and Botswana Guardian* to
read that only days hence Bophuthatswana will play host to a 'galaxy of
stars' for the opening of Sun City. My patient reader, if he has followed me
this far, may wish to skip this. I record it solely in the thought that in a
couple of hundred years, when the whites here have grudgingly let
themselves be assimilated into Azania (as Derek tells me the republic will
be renamed), some Fellini may wish to know what follies the late twentieth
century got up to. For Sun City, as its name implies, is nothing less than a
self-contained city, providing escape for thousands of people, a place, says
the *Mail*, where,

Day and night will have no meaning – no natural light but thousands of reflected
and refracted beams to illumine the mind-blowing vista. Set in an ancient volcanic
crater on the slopes of the Pilanesberg near Rustenburg, it's a fantasy world, a
conceit of the imagination which makes time and space fade into the cosmos . . .
80,000 bricks have been laid every day for 18 months . . . an entertainment bar

hangs over the central slot machine area like a Star ship, its amber mirrored perspex sending down sunbursts of light . . .'

And the dark cloud beyond the Limpopo was no bigger than a man's hand.

I left Mafeking on 7 December bound for the north. From here, Rhodesia Railways took over, and we passed from the racially segregated system of South Africa to the good old British class system. This stage of the journey was a 24-hour, 500-mile ride on the daily train to Bulawayo through the spacious and exhilarating veld of Botswana. Rhodesia Railways have run this service for many years now, but it was still curious to consider the presence of Botswanan customs on a Rhodesian train. After all, there was a war going on up the line, and Botswana was a front-line state sheltering guerillas of the PF. But in Africa railways transcend politics. This line is Botswana's lifeline; they would like it for themselves, and are negotiating to that end. But in the meantime they are very gentlemanly about it.

Larger in area than France, with a mere 750,000 people, Botswana is poor and unexploited. For many years after independence in 1966 this former British protectorate was one of the world's poorest nations (albeit one of the few democratic ones). But there has been a dramatic increase of wealth and urban population in the last fifteen years. Now that new copper, nickel, and diamond pipes have been discovered, the bush awaits the exploiters.

The train winds through the beautiful hills beyond Lobatse, and I witness a glorious sunset. The dark veld to the south-west gained a faint milky-white opacity; in the amber sky floated single clouds tinged with blood red and purple; the sun disappeared with astonishing speed in a blaze of vermilion, leaving a line of golden brown clouds along the horizon. Then just before it actually goes dark, looking up from the red band above the hills, the sky shaded into a violent deep blue where the first stars stood out. Magnificent. Now this is what I call train travel! Forget about air-conditioning and gold glass. Open the windows.

And there's the evening meal to look forward to, cooked on a coal-fired Aga in a tiny galley. And after dinner, what sensations to sit back to. The sounds and smells of the fringe of the Kalahari desert: bush fires, cattle trails, sweet grasses of the veld, the chatter of distant voices. Every small halt bringing its quota of new travellers and their goods, new bustle and talk.

It is eight o'clock and we arrive at Gabarone, the capital of Botswana. The platform is crowded with children and baggage, women in bright print dresses, miners in cowboy hats, pedlars and sellers of sweet corn and beer. It's Friday night and a lot of people want to go home for the weekend. The conductor is allocating sleepers and bedding in First and Second Class. He is surrounded by a struggling throng, most of whom are waving booking forms at him: Friday night is always packed and there's usually a fight for beds.

'Mr Jongwe? To Palapye, yes sir, three berths. We get there 3.15 in the morning. Mr Ubongwe? Motloutse River. Coach 18b. Mrs Chikerema? Are you Mrs Chikerema? Let's see: Francistown. Right, this way thank you.'

'Watch out for the girls if you're on till Francistown,' my Glaswegian steward grins a wicked grin, leaning out of the open window. 'It's pay night you see. Ay, these girls come down the corridors in First and Second knocking on the doors. Keep it locked. *And* sleep on your wallet. Fourth is full of ragamuffins and pickpockets.'

And of course the delight about the Bulawayo slow train is that, unlike South Africa, you and your fellow travellers are not segregated. You can spend the night meeting Khama princes, politicians, students, guitar players, card and dice hustlers, *and* ladies of fortune.

It's only ten o'clock, but people go to bed earlier than in Britain. I read for a while. Alex, a friend in Joburg, lent me Stanley's *Travels through the Dark Continent*. In 1879 Stanley wagered that the Europeans would carve up the whole of central Africa in twenty years, dividing it all neatly with boundaries. And they did. But could he have possibly foreseen a hundred years ahead? In his wildest dreams?

At six in the morning the steward brought round tea in Rhodesia Railways liveried tea cups, and a jug of water with which to wash. I lifted the blinds to see the bush still stretching interminably. For five hours the narrow single-track line runs through this thickly wooded country for mile after mile dead straight; a thread so tenuous and insubstantial that the traveller is in constant expectation of finding it washed away, or ceasing altogether in a pile of sleepers and the whitening bones of Victorian railway navvies!

There is time for egg and bacon before we get to Francistown at about 7.30. Francistown was the old capital after Mafeking. This was the centre of Africa's very first gold rush in the 1860s. It was over in ten years, though the last of the town's forty-five gold mines only closed in 1964. Now, those with the expertise work in South Africa.

At Francistown a group of about a hundred get off, men from the Joburg reef, with their bags, their wide-brimmed hats, their transistors and their swagger. As the train pulls out, they are dancing on the platform. Africa!

By 9.00 there is a different atmosphere on the train. The crew are armed. We are approaching the Rhodesian border. 'Jesus is Coming! Are you ready?' says the huge placard at the frontier post at Plumtree. There I meet my escort, Craig. Young, fit, trimly bearded with a gold chain round his neck and carrying a stubby sub machine gun, Craig is a typical 'Rhodie', a formidable drinker of Castle lager and a tireless chatter-up of women.

'No we never get blasé,' he tells me over the first glass of the day, 'people who get blasé usually get buried. You can never pin them down to a man-to-man situation because it's a guerilla war: they could be out there now, taking a pot shot at my beer. In fact if they hit my beer I'll be more annoyed than if they hit me.'

Typical Rhodie bravado. The bar is now mainly stocked with middle-aged men in shorts, fit and embittered. There is a fragile Dunkirk spirit among them as they wait for the end of their country.

The line has ascended to Plumtree and the border. Just into Rhodesia, at Coldridge, you catch a glimpse of mysterious pyramidal hills far away to the right above the bush. Then the track enters a region of enormous stones, some arranged in weathered piles precariously balanced on top of each other in gravity-defying pinnacles. This is the south-west edge of the Matopo Hills. We are almost at Bulawayo.

'Room 224, thank you Sir.' The 'boy', who was about forty, put down my suitcase. He wore an immaculately pressed white shirt with lapels, white shorts, socks and pumps. He came back with tea in old Victoria Hotel silver and insisted on taking away my crumpled shirts for ironing. Outside the window lay the flat green landscape of Bulawayo, a city of parks, palm trees, teak and jacarandas. Banks of black cloud were building up from the east. Big drops of rain struck the window panes. A crackle of lightning flashed over the perimeter and down to the darkening bush on the horizon. The electricity seemed to hang in the mouth like a premonition, sharp and acrid. On the bedroom desk was a copy of *Bulawayo This Month*: I opened it to read of the Toastmistress' Club; Scottish Country Dancing; the Matabeleland Dog Training Club. We cling to these reassuring arrangements of society. But how fragile they are. 'Refrigerated candles burn longer,' says the handy hints page. Rhodesia is still keeping its chin up.

The main story in the *Bulawayo Chronicle* tells of the expected fears about the now agreed ceasefire; the adverts show the underlying drift – the property columns are full of bargains ('4 servants qtrs, s/pool . . . chalet with bar, huge wendy house . . .'); the 'jobs wanted' page too ('housemaid, clean honest and v. reliable worker; present employer emigrating').

Bulawayo still has the feel of a pioneer town with its wooden sidewalks and its streets wide enough to turn a four-yoked ox-cart. In 1893 this was the site of the royal kraal of King Lobengula of the Matabele. But Rhodes coveted his mineral wealth – more perhaps than a through route to Cairo, though Rhodes' map in Bulawayo Museum shows his red crayon doodle right up central Africa. In 1893 the Matabele were overthrown and in 1897 the railways arrived here, 800 miles from Vryburg. So swiftly did the exploiters open up the heart of Africa. It is difficult to imagine the significance this had for the whites. It meant real contact for pioneers camped in hostile land, 'the beginning of civilisation in its entirety,' said the *Bulawayo Chronicle*, a new era for 'the men who have led England's advance into the heart of the Dark continent'. The commissioner for South Africa, Alfred Milner, called it a 'great day in the history of South Africa and the empire'. Three cheers for Joe Chamberlain! The banners said, 'Forward Rhodesia' and 'Our two roads to progress, railroads and Cecil Rhodes'. The omens were propitious. Even without the immense goldfield they hoped for, there was the greatest coalfield in Africa, and the magnificent soil of Rhodesia.

As for Lobengula, that 'naked old savage' as Rhodes called him, he died within a year of the conquest. Of smallpox, it was said, but if you read his disillusioned pleas to the great white queen in London, you may think like me that he died of a broken heart. Beaten in battle by Rhodes' mercenaries, the British South Africa Company Army, he was compelled to sign away his land in a famous peace parley celebrated by white Rhodesians as the founding of their nation. 'Their eyes wear a discarded look,' said a contemporary, 'their past is gone and they have no future.'

The Sunday after my arrival I was driven out to the Matopos by friends in spite of the restriction of petrol rationing and a four o'clock curfew. The place we sought is called 'view of the world', Rhodes' name for it. It is a great granite whaleback surmounted by huge balanced boulders. From the top there is a view round the whole circle of the horizon, the jagged rocky ranges of south-western Rhodesia. The Matabele thought it a magical place, the home of benevolent spirits. Here on the top now are buried

Rhodes, Jameson and Coghlan (the first prime minister), a trio of troubled spirits. At the bottom of the hill is a lodge which has a display of Rhodes' life in it, including a framed picture of Oriel College, Oxford, Rhodes' college and mine. 'Boss went to the same school as Mr Rhodes,' said my guide to the warden, helpfully. He nodded blankly. How long, I wondered, before the memory of Rhodes and his eponymous state vanishes here? (In fact, within a month of the election of 1980, his statues would be smashed all over the land.) Rhodes never saw his railway to the Falls completed. Here at the graveside Kipling spoke his epitaph: 'Living he was the land, and, dead, his soul shall be her soul.' And so it was to be – for as long as his Rhodesia lasted.

7.30 a.m., Tuesday 11 December. I came down to Bulawayo station to take the daily mixed goods and passenger train north to Thompson Junction. With me was Graham from Government Information. The emergency laws meant no journalist could go anywhere unsupervised. But Graham was a companion rather than a guard; middle-aged, laconic and discriminating, he had seen it all. The train was late. Under a veil of drizzle I watched a Rhodesian Garratt shunting in the sidings, a really spectacular sight this, 220 tons of locomotive giving out ferocious explosions of steam. By July 1980 steam here was to have been a memory. But in the last two years of the war the trend has been reversed. Rhodesia has large coal reserves, and steam engines are being rebuilt. In this way the Rhodesian government has been able to fight the shortage of foreign currency and oil under sanctions. There is even talk of building new steam engines, though the Manchester firm who made them, Beyer-Peacock, is long gone. Standing here in the rain on the day UDI was due to be lifted was a time to reflect on the position of Rhodesia's railways. They lie at the centre of the systems of southern Africa. From Bulawayo lines reach to all points of the compass: to the copper belts of Zambia and Zaïre through Victoria Falls, and on to the Atlantic at Lobito by the famed Benguela railway of Angola; to Lusaka and Dar on the Tan-Zam railway; to Beira and Maputo in Mozambique; into South Africa through Botswana and over the Limpopo at Beit Bridge. Most of these lines are now closed due to the war. With a black majority in Salisbury they could all operate again.

Our engine has arrived. It is a Garratt loaned by South Africa. Perhaps the one I saw all that time ago at Beaufort West? It carries extra water, and the passenger wagons are separated from the engine, for if the boys in the bush attack, they'll go for the driver first. We will make the 220-mile journey during daylight because of ZIPRA attacks; the guerillas have infiltrated much of the countryside by now. The train also carries troops. There is only a handful of passengers. But they all know what to do in an emergency. The women too.

'I know how to fire a machine gun,' said the pretty girl with the steady eye. 'I can take it apart, clean it and put it together again.' She seemed amused by my admiration: 'A lot of us have lost friends in this war. The bitterness between black and white won't be an easy thing to overcome. But in time we will. We've got to.' It was the most sensible thing I had heard so far.

Mid-morning we stopped at a place called Sawmills, sixty miles into the bush. There had been a derailment upline. So we just sat and waited. For six hours. We whiled away the time with the staff, Len (a Cockney) and Brian (a Yorkshireman), playing cards and discussing the merits of Yorkshire beers and holidays in Wakefield.

After the long delay at Sawmills darkness was coming on as we moved again. Another forty miles and we were on the Dett straight, the longest straight track in Africa which takes us seventy miles through the Wankie game reserve. As night came on and we slowly clattered along, animals appeared everywhere in the growing gloom: zebra, kudu, buffalo, sable, jackals, warthogs, giraffe and elephant. Looking out, the train appeared to be a tiny corridor of dimmed light in the vast velvet dark of the bush. For the first time I felt a sensation of the physical presence of Africa in all its mystery. I leaned back against the open window. An elephant trumpeted with a great screech yards from the train. I started. Graham smiled.

'In the old days,' he began, 'we used to take hampers of food and rifles and walk and camp in the Eastern Highlands around Inyanga and Leopard Rock. Now that is beautiful country. The Troutbeck Inn at Inyanga, or Mrs Hardy's old place at Rusape – she cooked the finest food in Rhodesia. Still does, though the 'ters got her housekeeper and put a grenade into her bar. One day you must see the east. Take the road from Chipinga to Umtali on the Mozambique border. In the spring the mountains are covered with red, musasa and mahogany; with yellow lilies, proteas . . . .' His eyes narrowed. 'Never be able to do that again, camping in the bush. Never in my lifetime at least. Mark my words there'll be 'ters in the bush for ten years after this war. This is a bloody hateful war. If the PF win – which they will – he'll never make them put down their guns. It's been their life for too long . . . .'

A colliery train at the mining town of Wankie

He looked up and blinked behind his tinted spectacles in the dim light of the saloon. He sipped his pink gin and shifted his battered old Browning into the corner. Outside, the train's headlight penetrated far into the night. The whistle blew a single long high blast.

It was midnight when we reached Wankie. Outside the carriage the rain was falling in torrents on a deserted platform; the end-of-November rains which reduce Wankie's stifling humidity to sodden jungle and streaming roads; November rains which bring an end to the killing season, as the Rhodesian army calls it, affording relief to the guerillas in the bush. Graham's driver was a lone figure in the pouring darkness. He drove us up to the promontory over Wankie where a giant baobab tree marked our hotel site.

In the morning in teeming rain I walked out almost naked to the end of the promontory to look over the drenched landscape of Wankie; coke ovens, cooling towers and pit heads dotted about the vegetation; a Barnsley in the bush, surrounded by undulating ranges of wooded hills under a low cover of grey cloud. Beneath me, skirting the hill, lay the line to Victoria Falls which I hoped to take the next day. There I caught a sight of another of the famed Rhodesian Garratts, a monstrous black engine with its detached front boiler like a bulbous nose, pulling a coal train towards the Falls which lay away in the rain and mist seventy miles to the north through the jungle. There was no longer a passenger service that way, because of the war. The line seemed tiny, dwarfed by the elements.

Wankie is southern Africa's biggest coal outcrop. It provides the government with the coal it needs to run industry and the railways and continue the war. It is a company town. Owned by Anglo-American, the overlords of de Beers, and therefore part of a big-business mineral empire which rules right up this railway line from the Big Hole at Kimberley, the Joburg gold reef, the diamond pipes in Botswana. This land went to de Beers as part of the deal for funding Rhodes' seizure of Matabeleland, and passed to Anglo-American in 1953. More than any other place, perhaps, this sustained the fifteen years of UDI.

That night Christopher Soames arrived to lift sanctions and pave the way for an election. He made a speech on the radio, prefaced by martial music and a full list of his honours to the last CMG. That night in the Wankie Miners' Club we watched *Coming Home*, a film about the Vietnam War. The audience applauded the patriotic sentiments of Jane Fonda's husband and hissed Jon Voight, the anti-war veteran. The love scene was cut by the censor. Afterwards in the bar miners from Sheffield and Doncaster supped their Lion lagers while a mine captain from Barnsley buttonholed me.

'Bloody great country this, lad. God's own country. Come back to England? You must be joking. Gone to the dogs, mate.' He looked me up and down. 'They don't know how to work there any more, especially the young 'uns.' Like many Rhodies this man had come out after the war, disappointed by the turn in English politics ushered in by Labour's victory in 1945. We didn't fight the war for that, they said to themselves. So they came out here to preserve the virtues they thought they were fighting for. Rhodesia still has the feel of fifties Britain. And it's true: if most Rhodies came back today they would be dismayed by what they saw. Now they are on the end of the plank.

In the bar while a pianist played 'My Way' Craig was holding forth in front of the girl we'd met on the train. He was depressed because a convoy car had been hit and four men killed near Vic Falls. Tomorrow while Graham and I rode an armed freight, he would be in a convoy.

'Look man,' he said, 'I guarantee we will get hit: no way we will not get hit tomorrow.' He still had his Rhodesian-made replica of a short Israeli tommy gun: 'I'll sit up front tomorrow, next to the driver, 'cos if the 'ters attack I'll want to spray 180 degrees, and if you boys are in the front seat I don't want to have to blow your effing heads off, man.' Suddenly I was glad I was going to be on the footplate.

Next morning in the yards at Thompson Junction by Wankie I boarded the footplate of class 15a number 395, a Beyer-Garratt bound for the Falls with a cargo of coking coal for Zambia and Zaïre. On the plate with me was a soldier, Bruce (a real gentleman, quiet, dignified), and the three-man crew, the furnace being hand-stoked. Graham was in the guards van with the guard and two black troopers of the Rhodesian army ('trust them with my life,' whispered Bruce). The most exhilarating journey of my life began at about 10.00 on 13 December, the day after Soames' arrival. The war was still going on. The previous night in Thompson Junction a shunter had been wounded and a train sprayed with bullets. In Wankie town a policeman had been killed. None of us really knew what to expect.

There are a dozen little halts between TJ and the Falls. Now they are deserted. One by one we passed them, Sambawizi, Nashome, Lobangwe, and not a sign of life at any of them. At midday we stopped at Matetsi to take on water and rake out the fire box. The previous day I had visited the military command for permission to go to Matetsi, and I knew that it lay in the heart of a guerilla zone. When we got there we found the army post sandbagged in at the river crossing. There was a small radio station behind high wires, and the water tank. Two men had been killed here last week. Bruce tied a bandana round his forehead to keep the sweat out of his eyes. The driver's mate perched on top of the engine and swung the gantry pipe round to the boiler, while Graham and the troops fanned out facing the silent bush. The sun was really hot by now, and the burning ash showering out of the fire box made it impossible to stand near the locomotive. The bush was invitingly green and shady, but Bruce said the paths were booby-trapped. I sat down on the rails until it was time to climb back aboard.

On the last stretch, the thirty miles to the Falls, we touched fifty miles an hour through beautiful broken country, vivid green bush with rocky gulleys traversed by water courses. Some trees were covered with blossom, others dotted with red fruit; there were baobabs, palms, and some trees which looked like oaks, elms and chestnuts. *Et in Arcadia ego*! Momentarily all thoughts of war receded. Then, at about five miles distance, we saw the tell-tale cloud of spray beginning to be distinguishable from the clouds. Exactly what Livingstone had seen in 1855.

We came in sight for the first time of the columns of vapour, appropriately called 'smoke', rising at a distance of five or six miles, exactly as when large tracts of grass are burned in Africa. Five columns now arose, and bending in the direction of the wind ... the tops of the columns at this distance appeared to mingle with the clouds.

We sped into the Falls zone past the wire fences of the minefield, under the blockhouse with its oil drums and sandbags on the road bridge checkpoint. Victoria Falls was then a defended zone – a 'protected village' for whites, as it were. Ironic to think of the white hoteliers and shop-keepers huddled round the Falls for safety. When the Falls were first discovered by Livingstone, no natives were found to be living within a radius of ten miles, as if respectful of its primordial force.

Vic Falls Station: neat, well-kept, overflowing with bougainvillaea and jacarandas, flower-boxes and mimosa. The white sign says Cape Town 2651 k/m, Beira 1534 k/m. Engine 395 wheezed to a halt. We staggered on to *terra firma* black-faced, unburned coal in our hair, hot, shaky and exhilarated. The journey was almost over.

The railways reached the Falls in 1904, and the tourist industry rapidly followed to make the most of the scene. The Edwardian Falls Hotel, where I was booked in, still preserves the old style: huge electric fans swishing in the dining-room; be-fezzed waiters, misanthropic monkeys munching mangoes in the palm court, bougainvillaea, mosquito nets, barbecues, sundowners, planters punch, marimba bands, tribal dancing, tea, toast and marmalade, egg and bacon. And always the roar of the Falls, invisible from the hotel but for the smoke merging with the sky above Rhodes' railway bridge.

The place was virtually deserted. Tourism was by now non-existent. Not surprising really, for there were only two ways of getting there now the trains didn't run: either you careered by convoy from Wankie, guns at the ready, or you took an old Viscount from Bulawayo and twisted down like a falling leaf from the cloud cover in tight circles on to the airstrip, constantly veering away from the Zambian side to cut down the risk of SAM missiles and sniper fire. Such precautions were taken everywhere after a Viscount was shot down over Kariba.

That evening before dinner the station master drove me up the Zambezi

A train on Rhodes' bridge which spans the Zambezi gorge

to the edge of the minefield. Gingerly, for after dark hippos walk the river road. We passed three big American-style motels, all deserted, musty, mildewed in the humid tropical air, their carpeted dance floors the haunt of snakes and insects. The Elephant Hills casino lay empty, hit by a stray SAM missile from Zambia. At sunset impala teemed at the water hole, temporarily returned to Africa.

We walked down to the river. The Zambezi looked like a great dark ocean. Harry picked up strange husks and fruit and told me how they grew. About to retire, he was weary and could not disguise the bitterness he felt about the fall of his country. He would not stay in Rhodesia if the PF won. I reflected that after all these years of war, the white Rhodesian nationalists lived in what was to all intents and purposes a police state. All their news was censored, for example. They had never heard Robert Mugabe speak! Harry shrugged and looked at me as if I was personally responsible for the Lancaster House sell-out, as he called it. We stood silent there in the forest like the characters in the Conrad novel, confronted by the stillness of the forest 'with its ominous patience, waiting for the passing of a fantastic invasion'.

There remained one last walk to complete the journey. The curfew lasted till 6 a.m., but I went down to the Falls at five to savour the moment. Dawn here rises over Zambia right behind Rhodes bridge, shooting streams of sunlight through the cascades and forming rainbows in the water vapour, above you, below you, and all around you. One of the few places on earth, perhaps, where you actually can be over the rainbow! By the gorge the rain forest grows out of itself, tangled creepers and saplings pushing through the sodden trunks of their dead progenitors: a mulch of rotten bark and leaves dotted with red aloes and dozens of orange butterflies. Wild animals are here too, warthogs, impala, gazelles, though all retire at dawn. In this fantastic moment I felt the ecstasy of a rain king, but my reverie was broken by the muffled boom of a landmine.

'Usually game, sometimes a 'ter,' said Craig when I got back for breakfast. 'The elephants break down the fences. Sometimes you get a whole herd of impala blowing themselves to pieces.'

Rhodes' graceful bridge still spans the Zambezi gorge, four hundred feet above the swirling maelstrom of the Boiling Pot. It was built by the Cleveland Bridge and Engineering Company of Darlington in 1903–4, prefabricated and pre-erected on their premises before being shipped out to Africa. The railway reached the Falls in 1904, and the bridge itself was opened the next spring. By then Rhodes had been dead three years. He had asked that the bridge be built so close to the Falls that the spray would wet the carriage windows. It does, I am told. But in December 1979 the only trains to pass over the bridge were Zambian, picking up our load of coal and maize. Like everyone else I was forbidden even to step on the bridge. In December 1979 this was the front line in Africa.

Over the gorge the Zambian frontier post surveyed us with binoculars. Had it not been for the war, I could have crossed the bridge and followed Rhodes' route northwards through Livingstone to Lusaka, Dar-es-Salaam, Mombasa, Nairobi, Lake Victoria, Kampala, Rejaf, then eleven days by boat to Juba and back on the train at Khartoum, Wadi Halfa, Aswan and Cairo. Rhodes' dream never actually became reality, though you can still travel 6500 of the 8000 miles by rail. Maybe I'll do it one day.

*   *   *

Now it all seems so long ago. The Blue Train still carries its cosseted passengers from the Cape to Pretoria. But steam is to end on the line from De Aar to Kimberley. The South African government has announced plans to give Soweto full city status and its own university; so Derek and Lucky will no longer be 'temporary'. Mafeking is no more. Rhodesia is now Zimbabwe, and Rhodesia Railways are the National Railways of Zimbabwe. You can travel once more by passenger train to Victoria Falls.

It is hardly a hundred years since the Falls were first seen by a white man. 'A scene so lovely,' Livingstone said, 'that it must have been gazed on by the angels in their flight.' In that time the tide of white colonialism has advanced and receded. It may already be too late for South Africa to respond to that tide. Like the Falls themselves the current of history is remorseless, unswerving, and deaf to persuasion.

AUSTRALIA

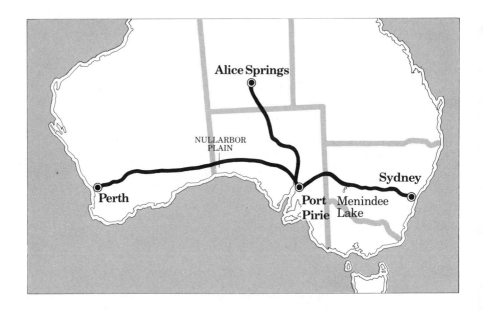

The Long Straight

MICHAEL FRAYN

Adapted and Edited by Dennis Marks

THURSDAY 5.30 A.M.

Two hundred years ago there was only one geometric line in Australia: the horizon that closed it off from the rest of the world. In the dawn twilight at the mouth of Sydney harbour, you can just for a moment catch the feel of how it was – a nameless place in a nameless year. The edge of a continent, without a geography and without a history; wandered but not settled, its words written on the wind and gone; a world without right angles or plane surfaces. Until at last, over that horizon, one southern summer's day came Europe and its hard shining reason. And all at once the nameless year is 1788 and the nameless place begins to become Australia.

This is where they came, the first thousand settlers, out of the Pacific and through Sydney Heads, out of the East like the rising sun. They had touched first at Botany Bay, the harbour that Captain Cook had discovered eighteen years earlier. But Botany Bay had not lived up to Cook's description of it. So Captain Phillip, their commander, set out to explore for himself. And a dozen miles to the north of Botany he hit upon Sydney Harbour.

It was the sun that brought them here, the sun and the pursuit of geometry. All the other coasts of Australia, north, west and south, had been discovered many years before. Ships in the East India trade had sighted and wrecked upon them; found them barren and apparently harbourless. Captain Cook discovered the east coast because he wasn't trading. He was in the Pacific on a scientific exploration. He was making observations for the Royal Society, trying to compute the distance between the earth and the sun.

The settlers landed in Sydney Cove, flanked now by the Harbour Bridge and the Opera House. This is where geometry and steel and the rules of harmony came ashore. The European mind in the person of 529 convicts together with the troops to guard and flog them. Their first act, when both men and women prisoners had been landed, was an orgy which was only ended by a thunderstorm. Over the next two years, their crops failed. Their animals wandered off into the bush and died, until only one sheep was left. The whole colony starved to death.

But in the end, the seed took, and from the soil of Australia came forth straight lines and rational curves. Rectilinear offices and hotels. The curve of freeways and the smooth arc of theatre and opera house. Solids of the most intricate and sophisticated geometry. And there was one line drawn from here that in the end stretched right the way across Australia. Human order and logic inscribed on the wilderness. The line of the Transcontinental Railway, and I've come to Australia to follow it.

THURSDAY 2.30 P.M.

From Sydney to Perth the line goes, two thin ribbons of steel, all the way across from the Pacific to the Indian Ocean on the other side, nearly 2500 miles. It took 120 years to build on and off. It crosses most of the history of Australia as well as its geography. I flew across last time I was here. Everybody said *then* that I should have taken the Indian Pacific. And Sydney Central Station is certainly encouraging. I bet they don't have an indicator with brass handles at the airport. And lovely old engraved glass doors that swing open on the command of a photo-electric cell. According to the timetable, the old train on one of the suburban platforms is called the Fish. And there's another one called the Chips. Have they got aeroplanes called the Fish and the Chips? Or photographs of resorts? I haven't seen photographs of resorts in years. I haven't seen carriages painted bright red and with jugs of water by the luggage racks either. And this charming, antique rolling stock is still in service on the suburban lines because the government have spent all the money on the shining stainless steel and air-conditioning that we're travelling in.

'Ladies and gentlemen. The Indian Pacific will depart at three fifteen. Will all persons not travelling kindly leave the train. Thank you.'

Aunts and uncles kiss unwilling children. The conductor checks his watch. The driver rolls a cigarette. I'm being seen off by a friend, Ross Campbell, a retired columnist like myself. He stands on the platform, peering in through the double glazing at me as I sit in the solitary splendour of my own room, or rather my own roomette, with its folding bed, folding washbasin and folding loo. A solemn moment.

'Anyway, thanks for everything, Ross,' I say.

'I think it's double glazing, isn't it?' he replies.

'I'm sorry, Ross, I can't hear you. It's double-glazed.'

'What?'

'No, cool, it's air-conditioned.'

'Don't mention it. It's been a pleasure.'

And at three fifteen precisely, 143 passengers, twenty-eight employees of New South Wales Railways, and a film crew move slowly out of Sydney Central Station. Three days. When you can fly it in four hours. We must all be mad!

It's a dinosaur, this train. Stainless steel and air-conditioned it may be, but really it's a sport, a throwback to the days of the Orient Express and the Great Cunarders. Five-course silver place-settings and glasses for fine wines, all gleaming in the afternoon sun.

And it's not a nostalgic survival. It's a brand-new train. It's only been running since 1970. At a time when the rest of the world was ripping up its railways, Australia was only just completing its first transcontinental line. At some little cost – the final seven years work came to 120 million pounds.

The first section was built as early as 1850. All suburbs now, working-

The Indian Pacific passenger express at Sydney terminal

class suburbs. Bungalows and factories. Stations with misleadingly familiar names – Stanmore, Lewisham, Croydon. The original line just went out to Paramatta, ten miles up the harbour, and already it looked like a dinosaur to some. The population was too small to support it, and anyway there was nowhere much for it to go. Settlement clung to the narrow coastal plain. It was a maritime colony, peopled and supplied and governed by way of the sea. At the beginning of the nineteenth century Australia stopped sharply thirty-five miles west of Sydney. And what stopped it was the Blue Mountains.

They are not very high, 1000 metres or so, but for years the combination of thick bush and sheer rock face made them impenetrable. Escaped convicts disappeared up into the hills in the belief that they were climbing through to China. It was only the drought of 1813 and the desperate need for more pasture to support the colony that drove the first explorers to try yet again. It is stockbroker belt now, I suppose, since the railway came through in the 1860s, but still densely forested with eucalyptus and dark ironbarks, still alive with birds as brilliantly coloured as children's comics. The first of the immense barriers that the interior presents.

These are the last hills we cross for 2400 miles. Hard country for the railway engineer. We're double-headed now, climbing one foot in thirty-three, and electric, at any rate as far as Lithgow. But in the 1830s it took tremendous virtuosity to get the line up to the summit of Mount Victoria, the high point, 1600 metres above sea level. We get down the sheer cliffs on the Western side these days by way of a chain of tunnels, blasted through the solid rock. But there was no money for that kind of tunnelling in the 1860s. So they brought the line down the cliff face in three tremendous swoops. The top one has been turned into a scenic motor road. You can just make it out on the left 100 metres above the Indian Pacific track. The old trains would come down the top stretch, stop at the buffers, switch the points and reverse down the middle gradient.

Railway enthusiasts have restored this section of the line, and they run their own train up and down it. Several trains and cheerful picture-book rolling stock, bought off Queensland Railways and lovingly looked after in the sidings between the middle gradient and the Indian Pacific line. Most of the drivers and firemen are professionals off diesels and electrics – a real busman's holiday. The Great Lithgow Zigzag, the first legend of Australian engineering. Zig in, zig back and zig on again, down the bottom gradient, where we round the curve of the mountains and run on down to Lithgow, our first stop.

This is where the electrics come off and the diesel takes over, because at Lithgow the wires from Sydney end. We're only ninety-seven miles out, but we're across the great divide. It seemed at the time like the bridging of the Mississippi in America. The impassable barrier had been passed. We leave Lithgow in the last of the evening sunlight, and the West lies open before us. Rich lands we're entering here. The first gold in Australia – that is what brought the settlers. Then the gold ran out and they stayed to farm – wheat, wool, fruit, vines. That's what brought the railway. They called it the

The Indian Pacific glides through the rich lands between Lithgow and Broken Hill

Westward Thrust, and they were thinking of the westward thrust across America. They imagined the railway going on for ever across the continent, and they were thinking of the Union Pacific racing across to meet the Central Pacific out of California in 1869. Banjo Patterson, the man who wrote 'Waltzing Matilda', was born just down the line near Orange. He talked about 'the vision splendid of the sunlit plains extended'. The vision splendid – and we're heading into the West after it, a straight golden line into the eye of the setting sun, over the horizon into pure conjecture.

And in the dining car, there's Golden Sponge Pudding. My favourite pudding! Show me the airline that has Golden Sponge! The vision splendid of the sunlit meal extended.

And after the sunlit meal, the first-class club car. Polished veneer and little tables with holes for the wine glasses. Very tasteful. There is even a piano. A bit like the senior common room in a rather well-endowed new university. But a university, it seems, for all the aunts and uncles in Australia. A fairly mature crop of adventurers here in the first-class club car, with a fairly mature taste in keyboard music . . . 'The White Cliffs of Dover', 'The Loveliest Night of the Year'.

FRIDAY 7.00 A.M.

'Good morning, sir. Cup of tea?'

The fertile plains didn't even last the night. Scrub. Red earth. A little parched grass. The great brown waterless waste. I wonder where it started. I wonder where it will end. Dust and spinifex and the huge eye of the sun. Railways of Australia have thoughtfully provided a strip map, but it's difficult to read in a five-foot-square roomette with a shaving brush in one hand and a razor in the other. Some sort of stream back there. Seven fifteen, it must be Menindee. My God, that was the Darling, one of the biggest rivers in Australia. I see why the great Australian explorers all grew beards. One glance in the shaving mirror and you might miss the only water for the next hundred miles. Heaven knows what's going by on the other side while I'm stuck here with soap on my face. And while I stare out of the right-hand windows at endless dust, the director stares out to the left at a sheet of blue water stretching to the horizon.

'Good morning, Dennis. Did you see the River Darling?'

'No. I saw the lake though.'

'Lake?'

'Lake Menindee.'

I knew you could never see anything out of trains. Out there, beyond the double glazing and air-conditioning, endless dryness. Heat that could kill a man in thirty-six hours. Inside, fruit juice, grapefruit segments, eggs – poached, boiled, fried – breakfast steak . . . My breakfast companions are the same second honeymooners who shared the dinner table with me last night. At every table, travellers stare out across the silver and the linen at the empty bush.

'Did you see those kangaroos this morning?' asks the wife.

'No.'

'I saw hundreds and hundreds of them.'

'We saw an emu.'

'Oh, I didn't see any emus.'

An elderly American lady stares at a patch of scrub.

'No. Just watch that clump of trees right there.'

'That's a lovely lot of bacon you've got there.'

'I saw something move. Now we've passed it and I didn't see that animal come out again.'

'. . . and two lovely eggs.'

Emus. Scrub. A world of dust. What must it be like living out there?

FRIDAY 12 NOON

One of the people who lives out there is Ron Adams. He works out of Broken Hill, our first stop on the second day. If you want to see anything for a hundred miles around Broken Hill, Ron Adams will take you there. He's employed by the New South Wales Department of Decentralisation as an Information Officer and he drives hundreds of miles in the bush every week. Ron is a fastidious man of about forty, who wears razor-pressed lightweight suits and neat ties, in temperatures of well over 100 degrees fahrenheit. He is a miner's son and a miner's grandson and an ex-miner himself. He's offered to drive me back to Lake Menindee. It's only 198 kilometres away – just round the corner! Ron is an expert on irrigation, dams, anything to do with water. You could say he has water on the brain.

'It's a challenge to pit yourself against the country, and the countryside here can be very hard. This is the dry arid country and this is the end of the summer, so you can see, if we don't get rain soon this is going to be a very, very dry winter.'

'Have you ever come across people who didn't survive in this country?'

'We've been fortunate as far as tourists are concerned, but what we have noticed is some locals have perished out here because they feel they know the country so well. They take these little risks, that everybody else is warned not to take, and that is their downfall. The main thing out in this area is to carry water. If you've got water you'll survive. If anything does happen, stay with your vehicle.'

The ocean had been a terrible enough barrier to cross – 12,000 miles, half of them through the Roaring Forties, but this ocean of land behind the mountains was even worse. In fact, it was impossible, even, for a start, unthinkable.

'Can we stop somewhere?' I suddenly ask.

'Where, Michael?'

'Anywhere.'

Over a curve of land in a cloud of dust and there is arid flatness to the horizon and beyond, a low frieze of hills in the far distance, 150 miles away. As Ron opens the car door the roar of the air-conditioning is drowned by the buzz of the insects.

'They breed plenty of flies here.'

Ron produces a can of Aerogard.

'Hold on, I'll give you a spray.'

One hundred and four degrees fahrenheit and wherever you look the ground is dry and yellow. In five minutes of walking Ron and the car and the trees by the roadside are simply dots in the landscape. Another five minutes and even the dots have disappeared. A blank. A nothing. For a long time it wasn't even Australia. The name didn't exist, there was no idea of Australia to be named. Cook called the land he found on the Eastern seaboard New South Wales. The British Government proclaimed that New South Wales stretched back to an arbitrary line of longitude down the centre of the continent. An undrawn line across an unseen land – to the East of the line, nothingness; the West, nameless nothingless.

And after another ninety miles of air-cooled emptiness, there it is, stretching away to the horizon, Lake Menindee.

'Water is the one vital aspect of development here, Michael. A lot of city people take water for granted. But with water out here you can do anything. At the present moment there's 18,000 acres of crops of anything from cotton to wheat and barley. The water here comes from the Darling. It's fed into the Darling basin from the Blue mountains and the river is stopped at the Darling Dam and moved out into these man-made lakes.'

Water. It is like one of those huge mirages that used to haunt the old explorers as they staggered from one dried-up creek to the next. The hope of water obsessed them: water to drink – and water to navigate. Because what they were looking for was the sea, the familiar, navigable sea, an inland sea on which they could sail across to the West. It was the River Darling that seemed to offer some hope. Oxley, Sturt and other explorers tracked the rivers down westwards from the Great Dividing Range, then lost them in impassable swamps or in the dry earth itself. But there was no outfall to be found on the coast; an inland sea was the only possible explanation. But in the end it was the River Darling that washed the theory away. Sturt found its junction with the Murray-Murrumbidgee system and traced it down to its mouth in the ocean, hidden on its seaward side by a deceptive sandbar.

But even after this, Sturt couldn't quite give up the dream. In 1844 he came back through Menindee on another expedition to the centre. He had eleven horses, thirty bullocks to haul the drays, 200 sheep to slaughter for meat, and he was hauling a boat. But what he found in the interior was not the sea. It was a desert so dry that the screws fell out of the boxes and the leads fell out of the pencils. In the end, it was water that brought the railway, back to Menindee from Broken Hill to serve the mines in 1919 and on to Menindee from Condobolin in 1927 to capture the wool traffic from the river steamers.

SATURDAY 10.00 A.M.

We are back on the Indian Pacific now, heading westwards from Broken Hill on the original track that carried first the silver, then the lead and zinc across into South Australia, down to the smelters at Port Pirie. Bit by bit, the line was drawn, backwards and forwards and with more rubbing out and redrawing than a child's geometry book. They had to rebuild the track down to Pirie to take the Indian Pacific – it was the wrong gauge. Well, we're out of New South Wales now and racing along the Flinders ranges into South Australia. Wooded hills. Pastures. This is really another Australia coming out to meet us. Australia as it grew didn't come overland like us. There was no railway, there was no road. Australia came round by sea and started out all over again on the coast, in Melbourne, in Adelaide, in Perth. Each new colony pushed out separately into the interior, under its own government and with its own ideas. About building railways, among other things.

Peterborough. Another familiar name, our first stop in South Australia. This is where the philosophies of Sydney and Adelaide come face to face. We're waiting on the westbound platform while the tractors unload baskets and boxes and parcels and shunt them over to the southbound Aurora. Our train runs on rails that are four foot eight and a half inches apart, the classic British standard gauge. It is said to be the distance between the wheels of a Roman chariot. The Aurora, the connection with Adelaide, the South Australian capital, runs on rails five foot three inches apart, the Irish standard gauge – probably the length of Brian Boru's sword arm. All the old main lines of South Australia and Victoria were built on the Irish gauge. The only way a train can run direct from Broken Hill to Adelaide is by being shunted into the works, jacked up off its wheels and getting a completely new set of bogies.

How did they manage to start off English at one end of the line and finish up Irish at the other? Well, it was rather like all the old music hall stories – there was an Englishman, an Irishman and a Scotsman. The Irishman was the engineer for New South Wales, and he persuaded everyone to standardise on the Irish gauge. Then they cut his pay and he resigned. But they didn't manage to inform the other colonies in time. That was Australia, separate communities, isolated from each other by distance, trying to co-ordinate their activities through the home government in London, 12,000 slow sea miles away. And the Englishman, well, I think it was an Englishman who persuaded South Australia later on in the nineteenth century to adopt the cheaper three foot six inch narrow gauge. The line from Broken Hill was narrow gauge until it was rebuilt for the Indian Pacific, and Peterborough was purely a narrow-gauge junction. One last surviving goods line carries narrow-gauge trains north from here. *Railways of Australia* says the sign, and separate railways they remain. Three systems have had to get together to run the train. That's why the Indian Pacific spends half an hour at Peterborough, because New South Wales have gone home and taken their locomotive with them. For the next 1300 miles or so, until Western Australia comes out to play, the train is hauled by Australian National Railways. ANR is federal, but so far only South Australia and Tasmania have unloaded their systems and losses on to it. Well, that's Australia – still.

When you come to think about it, the smooth stainless-steel Indian Pacific is like one of those bland joint communiqués they put out at the end of some difficult and protracted negotiations. It's an enactment of national unity, and like most such documents it's the product of many earlier drafts, many conflicting proposals and counterproposals. For instance, the original draft for a transcontinental line wasn't even east to west; it was north to south. It was to connect South Australia with Asia and the rest of the world. But this first manifesto on wheels was such an extraordinary tangle of compromises, such a confusion of grand ideals and local expediency, that it's difficult to follow where it thought it was going from one mile to the next.

MONDAY 3.00 P.M

It set off north in 1878, and we're following its route, our train belching steam into the South Australian woodland just like the first transcontinental express. While the Indian Pacific presses west towards Port Pirie and Port Augusta, I've taken the weekend off to follow the original transcontinental up to Darwin. The aim, said the governor of the colony, when he cut the first sod, was to open up trade with India, China and Siam. This section of the line is steam-hauled these days, not because of ANR's bank balance, but because local steam enthusiasts have restored it, and it's not going north at all, it's going east, making a slight diversion on the way to India to pick up copper from the mines in the Flinders. But in fact it was so costly building a railway through the hills that it gave up and turned back without ever reaching the mines. Just as well really, because the copper mines all went bust.

The line staggered back to the plains to carry wheat from the great new wheatlands opening up around the oddly named settlement of Government Gums. In fact they were so hopeful of the line's prospects that they renamed the place Farina. A loss to the fine placenames of the world but perhaps just as well for the historical record, because there turned out to be no rain here in dry years and if it didn't say Farina on the map now, I'm not sure anyone would ever guess they had tried to grow wheat on those plains. So the line gave out once more. The restored track ends at Quorn, once the junction for passengers travelling through from Adelaide to the north. Now the trains for the north bypass all these early meanderings and Quorn is left high and dry, its hopefully named Transcontinental Hotel still waiting for the weary maharajahs and the thirsty spice traders.

MONDAY 11.30 P.M.

All the same, there is still a train running north along the old line. At Marree station, just before midnight, a whole interstate express is being shifted bit by bit across the platform by arclight. Bags and crates and tins of Fosters and half-eaten turkeys and thirty-two boxes of filming equipment. Because Marree, 180 miles north of Quorn, is where the new standard-gauge line ends and you change on to the old original narrow-gauge track, for the most famous train in Australia. The posters call it one of the 'last railway adventures' – the Ghan.

The same wiggly corridors, the same fold-down plumbing. All human life is here too, but it's slightly more antique, brass and mahogany. However, what the Ghan is chiefly famous for is its speed. The train leaves Marree at midnight on Monday, give or take a couple of hours, and according to the timetable, it's due at Alice Springs at 9.00 a.m. on Wednesday, a schedule which means maintaining a cracking seventeen miles per hour.

But circumstances often conspire to delay this ambitious programme. The ground is so dry here that the track is laid directly upon it, without ballast. Unfortunately, though, this is the floodplain of Lake Eyre, and when the waters *do* come they wash the sand away from under the rails. Then the train comes to a halt, sometimes for days, occasionally for months. Sometimes the wind blows the sand *over* the rails. Sometimes the train has been halted by plagues of grasshoppers and woodlice. There is a story about a woman on the Ghan who keeps asking the conductor what time they get to Alice Springs. Every time the train stops she asks him. The conductor gets a little impatient. 'What's the hurry?' he says. 'We'll get there some time in the next few days.' So the woman says: 'Listen, I'm due to have a baby.' 'Well,' says the conductor, 'you shouldn't have got on the train in this condition.' And the woman says: 'When I got on the train, I wasn't in this condition.'

TUESDAY 12 NOON

Edwards Creek. There is no creek at Edwards Creek this autumn. Like every other stream along the route, it's bone dry, and water is pumped up from the mile-deep artesian basin. A pumping tower and two shacks – the only human artefacts outside the train since dawn. The Ghan stops here to take on water and we're only three hours behind schedule. When you look back at the track we're travelling over, you can't help wondering if seventeen miles an hour isn't reckless bravado. Dry rot and white ants are disturbing the sleepers in their beds. The geometry is melting and buckling in the sun. On the rails go, though, on into the heart of Australia, staggering and weaving like two exhausted explorers, due north into the eye of the noonday sun. Over cracked earth and drunken bridges with nothing but rotting sleepers between us and the dry creek bed, sixty feet below.

The Ghan – an odd name, short for 'Afghan', because before there were cars and lorries in Central Australia, there were camels. They imported them originally for the building of the first overland telegraph line, along the same route as the railway. They spread and multiplied; caravans of camels converged on the railhead at Marree from all over the centre. In fact, Australia now exports fine thoroughbred racing camels to the Arabs. It was the camels that carried the rails and sleepers to build this line. The Afghans were the camel drivers they imported to look after the beasts. They were all called Afghans, of course, because they came from almost everywhere except Afghanistan.

The coaches are German for some reason. They look as if they were built for the Kaiser. The first-class club car is even more like a senior common room – Heidelberg University, perhaps – with its maple veneers of Schloss Wilhelmsthal and its moquette bucket chairs. In fact, the rolling stock was commissioned only thirty years ago for the east-west line, and it sits uncertainly on its narrow gauge bogies, rocking gently from side to side like the *Queen Elizabeth*. And a slow, soothing, timeless world it is, more like an ocean cruise than a train journey. Scrabble. Snapshots. Chess. Americans discuss their holidays in Russia. Australians complain about the price of drinks in London.

'This is the last call for the first sitting of lunch.'

Boeuf Stroganoff. Roast Lamb and salad. Queen of puddings. *Queen* of puddings. A cruise across an ocean of land, with nothing much to mark our passage except the lonely graves of the men who died building the line and a glittering wake of old beer bottles and cans.

TUESDAY 3.30 P.M.

We're stopping again. Greenfly? Grasshoppers? No, Oodnadatta. They let the passengers off here for twenty minutes to stretch their legs and take photographs. Aboriginal children stare at the travellers, and the travellers stare at the children. Two white-haired ladies from the Sydney suburbs strike up a conversation with the Aboriginal girls waiting on the station platform.

'How old are you?'

'Eighteen. She's fourteen.'

Between the two dark-skinned girls sits a ruddy-faced two-year-old child with wheat-coloured hair.

'Is that your little girl? You're lovely, aren't you. Little girl or little boy? Hasn't she got lovely blonde hair?'

'Little boy.'

'Where did she get all that blonde hair? Was his father blonde? Well, that's how he has blonde hair.'

What brought the line here? There's no copper. There's no water. It was unemployment, mostly. It was something to keep people going in the depression of the eighties.

A hundred yards away, on the other side of the track, skinny dogs worry broken bottles and flies worry the dogs. A couple of Aborigines scratch in the shade.

'I was in Fiji and if you know anything about the Fijians, how they have dark curly hair. Well, there was this little child and its hair was as blonde as blonde could be . . .'

The dogs sniff off towards the Transcontinental Hotel. We haven't lost hope yet. Straight on for China – at seventeen miles an hour. Students from the economy carriages are singing folk songs in the first-class club car. One hand cupped to the ear, the other clutching the book of lyrics. The Ghan used to take stockmen up from South Australia to Alice Springs for the cattle roundup. Now it carries botanists and retired mining engineers and mothers with unmarried daughters on bush holidays. A couple of teachers are taking their car to Darwin for a two-year drive round the Australian coast. The last great railway adventure.

Not for much longer though. They are just about to rip the whole track up and sell it to the Japanese for scrap. That's why they are letting it run down. It's being replaced by a new line, further over to the west, in November 1980. They're still rubbing out, still redrafting. But the most characteristic readjustment of all in the line's northward trek is that two days or so in from the coast, halfway across Australia, it creeps through a gap in the Macdonnell Ranges and expires in Alice Springs.

WEDNESDAY 3.00 P.M.

Somewhere at last and only six hours later. But it's an odd place to build a railway to. A few dozen streets, twenty or so pubs and a couple of aboriginal art galleries. It's the middle of nowhere, the first town in the Northern Territory, the emptiest state in all the empty Commonwealth of Australia. But then, that's the point of Alice Springs. That's why the two biggest buildings belong to Trans Australian Airlines and Ansett. That's why the tourists come here, to see what nowhere looks like. And if you want to see nowhere, you have to start somewhere.

In fact, Alice Springs became somewhere for a very simple reason:

because the railway ends here. Before the line arrived in 1929, this area had a white population of forty. And the railway ends here because if it wasn't going to reach the north coast, and it wasn't, and if it was going to end in the middle of nowhere, and it was, then it had to end – well, somewhere. And this place was already more somewhere than anywhere else because there was a repeater station on the overland telegraph, now preserved as a museum. They built the repeater station here because, in a dried-up creek just outside what is now Alice Springs, they found a waterhole, a puddle of river left over from the previous wet season. And in the parching Australian summer of 1980, even the puddle has dried up, only the waterline remains. Eight hundred miles at seventeen miles an hour to reach a dried-up waterhole.

WEDNESDAY 5.00 P.M.

The middle of nowhere; and if you're going to be anywhere in nowhere, there's a certain appeal to being in the middle of it, which is almost exactly where Alice Springs is. To be accurate, the dead centre of Australia is Mount Stuart to the north, but for tens of thousands of tourists every year Australia comes to a point in a strange bald bulging navel 260 miles to the south-east. Ayers Rock. After Sydney Opera House and the Great Barrier Reef, it's the most famous object in Australia. The trains don't run to Ayers Rock, but there are tourist buses, two daily Connair flights and four motels to look after you when you arrive. And the best way to see this huge red pebble, eight miles wide and a mile high, is from above in your own light aircraft – which is how Irwin Chlanda sees it, and photographs and films it two or three times a week.

Irwin is an Austrian, from Vienna. He's chief reporter on the local newspaper in Alice Springs, and when he isn't writing leading articles or filming news stories, he's piloting a Piper Lance or relaxing with a spot of sky-diving. Journalists in Central Australia hire planes like other reporters hire taxis.

'Are all the tourists who come here going to damage the landscape?' I ask.

'Well, it looks to be a very tough landscape, but it's not. It's very fragile. For example, around the other side of the rock there is a creek bed, quite a noticeable one, perhaps two metres wide and half a metre deep, which wasn't there before. It's simply there because people have walked over the ground and they've created a very slight depression, then the water has cascaded off the rock and washed it out. Now there's a creek bed at Ayers Rock that didn't exist before. Another example is what happens if people wander around picking up firewood. Beetles live in the dead trees, birds nest in them. When they decay, they fall to the ground and ants live in them. The excreta of these ants produce fertiliser. So if you pick up a twig or a branch that has fallen off a tree and burn it, it means that you deprive that small patch of the soil of its fertilisers for years to come.'

'What do the tourists do when they get here?'

'They look at the aboriginal cave paintings, some of them climb the rock and all of them photograph it.'

The special place for photographs, as sacred to the tourists as the rock itself is to the Aborigines, is called the Sunset Strip. The guide tells them when the rock is exactly the right shade of red and hundreds of shutters click in unison. Then they all get up at dawn on the following morning and wait to capture exactly the right shade of orange from another sacred site. Someone once rushed up ten minutes too soon, shouting 'Now!'

Tourists and cattle, the economy of Alice Springs. They ship the tourists in and they ship the cattle out, on their one-way journey back to Port Augusta, whence we set off for Alice last Monday night. And where the next Indian Pacific is due at 6.15 p.m., getting on with the business of crossing a continent. The original transcontinental line died in the desert like an exhausted explorer. By then – the late 1920s – the new transcontinental line had already struck out from Port Augusta westwards. It wasn't going to India or China or Siam. It wasn't going to pick up copper or silver or cattle. The Indian Pacific runs west from Port Augusta for purely political reasons, to tie Australia together. The line was planned when the colonies federated in 1900. It was the inducement to Western Australia, remote and isolated on the far side of that great sea of nothingness, to enter the federation. The work finally started in 1912, after Western Australia had threatened to secede from the new commonwealth. The vision splendid, here if nowhere else.

MONDAY 7.30 P.M.

Fillet of schnapper, roast turkey. My dinner companions left Sydney yesterday afternoon, I've lost count how long I've been travelling. But by midnight the Indian Pacific will be halfway across Australia. They don't know what travelling is.

The Indian Pacific heads out over the Nullarbor Plain

Low saltbush, parched infertile limestone soil. A dry ocean in a flat calm. The Nullarbor Plain.

'Cup of tea, sir?'

Null arbor – no tree. The great treeless plain. Five hundred miles across, with no trees, no hills, no valleys, no rivers, no towns, no villages. Nothing – except a single geometrical line: the railway itself.

'Ladies and gentlemen, the first sitting for breakfast has now commenced . . .'

For three hundred miles across the Nullarbor, it runs dead straight, the longest straight railway line in the world, a pure mathematical projection.

Breakfast. And whist. And knitting. And holiday snaps. One passenger train a day, loaded with old age pensioners, and all built for our benefit. Funny to think that's what it has come down to – plain economics. It's cheaper to fly across Australia than go first class by train, unless you're a pensioner. If you get the pensioners' concessionary rate you can go all the way first class for £100, a lot cheaper than flying economy. In fact every trip loses the railways £20 a head. Even the economy class is half full of students travelling cut price. Freight is what makes the money. The travellers on the Indian Pacific are really an irrelevance, symbolic passengers on a political diagram.

TUESDAY 9.00 A.M.

Endless flatness. Two straight steel threads stretching to the horizon. It's going to be a long day. In fact it's going to be an hour and half longer than yesterday – at Cook, we put our watches back to Western Australian time. Longer still for the driver. Every ninety seconds of his seven-hour turn of duty he has to put the vigilance control back, a dial with a needle and a red danger sector. If the needle goes over the 30-second mark into the red, bells ring and lights flash and the emergency brakes go on.

ANR have let me up into the driver's cab, where the diesel engine hammers just below the pain threshold and the driver squats with one hand on the dead man's handle and the other on his tobacco tin.

'How many times do you press that vigilance control in seven hours?' I ask.

'Work it out for yourself – every ninety seconds.'

'My God, that's something like 400 times. Do you ever fall asleep on this stretch?'

'Oh no, we're not allowed to do that.'

From Cook at seven thirty to Rawlinna at one, all the driver sees are telegraph poles and two straight lines that meet at infinity.

'How far ahead do you reckon to see a headlight?'

'In the daytime, three to four mile.'

'And at night?'

'Anything up to twenty odd mile.'

'I see there are a lot of nests in the telegraph poles.'

'Yes, they're the only sort of trees we've got around here for the crows to nest in.'

'I can't think what the birds did before they built the railway line.'

'They must have had trouble.'

When King O'Malley, the minister for home affairs, was fighting to get the money for this line, he prophesied to Parliament:

Before many years have rolled by, the country will hold a very large population, larger than ever crowded within the gates of Athens when her fighting men under Miltiades won liberty for humanity at the field of Marathon, larger than that of Sparta . . .

Was that another crow's nest?

. . . larger than Rome . . .

So far there are only the fettlers – the men who maintain the railway. They still call these little settlements camps. Before the war, the courts in Adelaide would withhold sentence on condition the offender came out here to one of these camps and worked for the railways. It was a kind of latter-day transportation. Even two or three years ago, someone who had worked out here told me, these places were refuges for people who had run away from their debts or their wives. They are the last of the Australian colonies. Half a dozen low clapboard houses and perhaps a water tank every fifty kilometres between Ooldea and Rawlinna. There is no television and the sun spoils the radio reception during daylight. It must have been a bit like this in Sydney at the very beginning, for ever waiting for supplies and news from over the horizon. Once a week they come, on the Tea and Sugar. Officially, it's called the Slow Mixed and it brings the water and the fuel, the groceries and the fresh meat. Every fortnight it brings the pay envelopes; every month, medical check-ups and playgroup; every six months, clothes and radios and toys and guns. The social workers who travel with the train tell stories of women in the camps having nervous breakdowns and wandering off into the bush. Just staring at it for seven hours numbs the mind.

TUESDAY 1.00 P.M.

Rawlinna and the first bend in the geometry since dawn. And the first tree. The driver is relieved here and the guard is waiting to let me back on to the train. He turns out to be a Pom – from Skipton in Yorkshire – and he plans to retire early in a couple of years' time and live off his gold mine.

'You've got a gold mine?'

'A small one – about 100 miles outside Kalgoorlie.'

'Tell me about it.'

'I'll take you there, if you like . . .'

Gold. The gleam of light from underground. It shaped Australia almost as much as the golden sun above; gold and the hope of gold. In the middle of the last century, when the first big gold strikes occurred, it trebled the country's population. It scattered people out of the cities into the bush. They walked 200 miles and more up from the coast to the goldfields in the nineties, pushing their belongings in wheelbarrows. In time, the track sketched by the prospectors became the solid line of the railway. It was the railways that brought Dave McCarten the guard to Kalgoorlie, but it's gold that keeps him here:

'It's what I'm here for, so I like to talk about it and I like to hear about it. They call it the sun metal. It's been there all the time – ever since man's been about, he's been after it.'

'Have you ever had a bar of gold out of your own mine?'

'A small one, about seventeen ounces and four grammes.'

'And you actually held the bar?'

'And photographed it and kissed it.'

The shift on the Indian Pacific is one week on and one week off, so every other week, Dave loads his utility wagon and takes his wife and his children and his dog 150 kilometres into the bush. This week Dave is on leave and he has an extra passenger in his 'ute'. He's invited me out to his place in the country for a barbecue and a spot of prospecting. The route takes us across the history of the prospecting West. Gold fever once raged across this part of Australia and the empty bush is still full of ghostly traces. Kanowna was a town of 12,000 people. Gone – every brick and rafter of it. Broad Arrow – 2000 people, eight pubs, two breweries and a stock exchange. Gone. There were 2000 people in Ora Banda as well. The public house is all that's left, the last thing to disappear, like the grin on the face of the Cheshire Cat.

But now with gold at 600 dollars an ounce there are prospectors out in the bush all around again. Some of them, like Dave McCarten, just come out at weekends, or during holidays. Others live out here and work at it full time. They watch each other like hawks. They note every new scratching in the earth. They reopen old workings and go through the old spoil heaps. The whole landscape is charged with possibility.

'Down in Paddington, there was a man and his fiancée, they went out driving together and when they came back they had fetched two or three bucketfuls of dirt. In the dirt was somewhere like 150 ounces of gold. It was two or three days before they were setting off on their honeymoon. They went to Melbourne and the miner caught pneumonia there and died, and his wife could never find the place again. And as far as I know, the place has never been found. I've been and looked myself.'

WEDNESDAY 1.30 P.M.

Dave McCarten's empire – the Double M mine on the Black Cat claim. A corrugated-iron shack nailed together from old cyanide drums from the State Battery. Cyanide is used to break down the ore-bearing rock. Dave's shack has a number 17 on the door.

'Number 17?'

'Seventeen the Bush.'

'It's quite cosy, number 17. Two beds, curtains, wallpaper.'

'What I don't understand is how you ever found this place.'

'Well, we got a book of cancelled gold mining leases, and looked for one with a low tonnage and high ounceage. This one was approximately $9\frac{1}{2}$ ounces to the ton.'

'That's quite high, isn't it?'

'That's rich, yes.'

'How much would you have to get out of it to make it worthwhile?'

'I'd have to take out at least two ton. That would give us an income of about 500 dollars a week. It's non-taxable, see, you don't pay tax on gold at all.'

'Is there anyone here who's not interested in gold?'

'They're not interested in gold, they're interested in money. It's a gold mining town and it's got everything because it just keeps on producing. By all accounts, there's more left in the ground than has ever come out.'

WEDNESDAY 8.00 P.M.

Nearly there, thanks to gold. It set the final seal on the Commonwealth of Australia. It was the goldfields that brought the line the last few hundred miles and it was the miners that voted Western Australia into the federation. Gold and then iron – the iron ore deposits in Koolyanobbing made it worthwhile to replace the old narrow gauge line ten years ago.

The Indian Pacific pulls in with only 400 slow miles to go. The waiters, cooks and barmen all leave the train. No more fish entrées and breakfast steaks. Bar stewardesses in neat red suits are all we need to look after us until Perth at seven tomorrow morning.

THURSDAY 6.30 A.M.

'Good morning, sir. Cup of tea? We should be in Perth by 7.00.'

Hills again. The Darling ranges behind Perth, like the Blue Mountains behind Sydney. Another Australia reaching back from another sea. Out of the rising sun, down from the hills, past the Swan River and into the rich coastal plain. A mirror image, beyond the great emptiness, a humanised landscape once more, with vineyards, comfortable outer suburbs, commuters with offices to go to and trains with small aspirations to get them there. Even the muddle of industry looks familiar after the Nullarbor. The human race is in control again, if only round the edges. It feels like home; it also feels as if it might suddenly disappear again and leave nothing but dust and scrub.

Perth Terminal. As bright and brand new as Sydney Central is cosy and comfortable, the lady from the car rental company with her bright professional smile, shining trolleys and sparkling telephone booths. I ring my friends here.

'Hello. It's me, Michael, I've arrived – I think.'

Two thousand miles down the track and a city as rich and towered as Sydney at the end of it. Hard-edged buildings fringed with palms, the grid of motorways and car parks. Like Sydney, it started off as a disaster. They had to beg the British Government for a supply of convicts at one point, just to keep going. All the wealth of Perth is new, it's minerals; huge deposits of iron ore above all. Western Australia is being moved ton by ton to Japan. Turned into Hondas and Toyotas and Datsuns. And of course shipped back again. It's so rich here, there's even talk of seceding again.

From the roof of the Allandale, you can see the city reflected in the Swan River and the freeway snaking off to the west, to the surfers of City Beach and the setting sun mirrored in the Indian Ocean. Mirror images. Another shining new city – but only after such a huge and ancient emptiness. Another shining silver river – but only after such a vast breadth of unwatered dust. Another ocean. Indian Pacific. It's a good name. From the Pacific to the Indian Ocean, one straight human line from the sunrise to the sunset. One thin straight scratch through the dust, marking it for rational man. And all the rest of it looking much as it must have done when those first settlers, with their geometry and their shackles, came round the bend of the world.

AMERICA

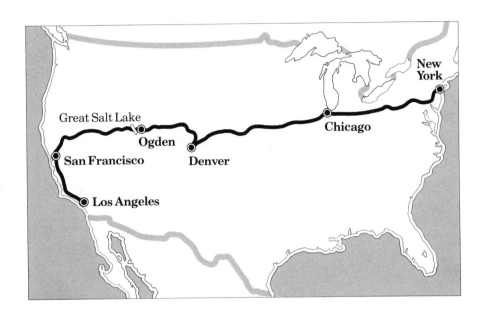

Coast to Coast

LUDOVIC KENNEDY

DAY ONE

'The Broadway Limited' – the voice of the Amtrak announcer reverberated throughout Penn Station – 'stopping at Harrisburg, Altoona, Pittsburgh, Lima, Fort Wayne, Gary and Chicago, is now ready to receive passengers on Track 14.' Town and cities were reeled off as casually as stopping-places on a London bus. But the overnight journey would take eighteen hours and cover a thousand miles.

Pennsylvania Station, in the heart of Manhattan, covers 125 square acres and used to be one of the great railway termini of the world. Once it was headquarters of the famous Pennsylvania Railroad, the so-called 'best gentlemen's club' in Philadelphia. A score of crack expresses left here every day for points west and south. But today it does not look or even feel like a railway station at all; more like a lower-level shopping precinct, a

81

The *Pennsylvania*, a private coach built for the president of the Penn Railroad

sanctuary from the hubbub of 34th Street up above. The concourse, which once resembled the nave of a Gothic cathedral, is now all glass and chrome. The ticket sellers sit behind plate-glass windows, as in a bank, and communicate with the sales office in the basement by means of a computer terminal.

For only $309.50 I bought a ticket to take me the 3000 odd miles to Los Angeles, three nights and four days away; and as I did so I felt that sense of keen anticipation that marks the beginning of any long-distance journey. What did The Broadway Limited – and the San Francisco Zephyr and the Coast Starlight which I would take later – have in store? As the old hymn says of Heaven:

> What joys await us there?
> What radiancy of glory?
> What bliss beyond compare?

The Broadway Limited is so called, not because it starts its journey within spitting distance of New York's theatreland, but because of the width of the permanent way, four parallel tracks built by the Penn Railroad to carry their passengers and freight over the Alleghenies to the west. It's now one of only two expresses which leave New York daily for Chicago. The other survivor, The Lake Shore Limited, goes north along the Hudson and crosses the Adirondacks near Albany. When I last came this way thirty years ago, it was in the crack Twentieth Century Limited. ('Limited' incidentally means limited in the number of passengers that may

be carried.) The Twentieth Century, like so many of its lesser competitors, is now extinct, a victim of the glut of motorways and jumbo jets.

At 3 p.m. the Broadway pulled out of Penn Station, and after a brief glimpse of the Manhattan skyline we were under the Hudson River and into the darkness of the Weehauken Tunnel. In the early days the line to the west began in New Jersey, on the other side of the Hudson. When a fellow Scot, Robert Louis Stevenson, made this same journey to California in 1879, he began his journey by ferry.

Stevenson, who travelled in an immigrant train, wrote an account of his journey called *Across the Plains.* For him and his fellow-passengers living conditions were spartan; hard wooden seats and, at night, bedboards; scratch meals snatched at station restaurants, and always some joker to shout that the train was leaving before in fact it had. Today you can choose between a reclining seat, a roomette where the seat turns into a bed, or a miniature bedroom; and for meals there is a well-appointed restaurant car which serves three courses and wine for around ten dollars a head. There were 178 of us on board the Broadway, half a train full. Yet so well has Amtrak succeeded that, had we been making the trip in mid-summer, we should have had to book two months beforehand.

For the first hour or so the train cut a swathe through the industrial landscape of New Jersey; derelict buildings on one side, the crowded freeway on the other. I went along to that most American of institutions, the club car, and joined a group of salesmen returning to Harrisburg from a convention in New York. 'They just did away with five trains,' said one man, 'but it's still cheaper to use the train with its lousy service than to drive. You know how much car storage costs in New York? Twelve dollars a day. That's right. You take the train, get in a cab and in fifteen minutes you're in any hotel you want. Only trouble with the trains is they're never on time. They don't try to accommodate you, they try and *de*commodate you.'

This is true enough; but if it hadn't been for Amtrak, it's unlikely that today there would be any long-distance passenger trains at all. In the fifties, when air and automobile travel came into their own, the big railroad companies began to go bankrupt one by one; and it was the collapse of the Penn Railroad at the end of the sixties which at last led government to take an interest. In 1971 a bill authorised Amtrak to take over the country's long-distance passenger trains. Like British Rail, Amtrak is now the butt of a thousand jokes.

Amtrak's problem is that with the exception of a few hundred miles of track between Washington, New York and Boston, it does not own the lines on which its passengers run. In the old days the crack expresses always took priority over freight; today, because freight is profitable and passengers are not, it is the other way round. Nor are matters helped by Amtrak's ancient, inherited equipment. The carriages that took us to Harrisburg were thirty years old, the electric locomotive that pulled them nearer fifty. No wonder that trains seldom arrive on time.

As it happened, there was a physical reminder on this journey of the Penn's happier past. The last coach on the train was the private coach *Pennsylvania*, built fifty-one years ago as a perk for the President of the Penn Railroad. Those were the days when what used to be called 'private varnish' was the ultimate in millionaire status. Today the Pennsylvania is owned by a New York lawyer, George Pins, whom I joined in the car's comfortable drawing-room cum observation car.

'I think there are certain things in life,' said George Pins, 'that one looks at and says "I'm going to have that", whatever the cost may be. I saw this car by chance, but I immediately resolved that I was going to be the person who would restore it and operate it in the grand tradition of American railroading.'

The *Pennsylvania* consists of dining-room and galley, master bedroom and shower, two other bedrooms and drawing-room. The decor is thirties'; vacuum flask by the bed, cushions in the livery of the Penn Railroad. Among those who have hired it (complete with cook and steward at around

500 dollars a day) are an advertising firm and a group who took it on holiday to Canada. President Kennedy and his wife rode in it to see the annual Army-Navy football game in Philadelphia. And it took Bobby Kennedy's body (accompanied by his widow Ethel and his brother Ted) on its last journey from New York to Washington.

'Nevertheless,' says George Pins, 'it's a big loser, and I'll probably soon be selling it. However nice it looks, there are appliances which must be kept in safe operating condition. They shake and rattle all the time and are expensive to maintain. It's like an old house that vibrates. You have to love it.'

As the sun set, we approached the Susquehanna River (the beauty of whose name, said Stevenson, equalled the beauty of the countryside) and just before seven we glided into darkened Harrisburg, Pennsylvania's capital. Here, at a cost to Mr Pins of 120 dollars, the *Pennsylvania* was unhitched from the Broadway and parked on Track 24. At dinner (Prime Ribs of Beef au Jus) we were joined by a legendary figure from the annals of American railroading, Rogers E M Whitaker, better known to readers of the *New Yorker* as E M Frimbo. Rogers, now eighty-two, is generally acknowledged to be the world's leading railroad buff. On tracks all over the world he has travelled more than 2,500,000 miles. But he is not optimistic about the future.

'It now takes two days and two nights,' he said, as we slurped mulligatawny soup, 'to travel from Chicago to Seattle by rail. That's the same amount of time that it took twenty years ago. It has not improved because of the miserable schedule, brought on by the miserable state of the track, by the miserable state of the equipment and by a certain number of miserable employees.'

As a young man Rogers spent his vacations working on the railways as a waiter. When Amtrak was formed he was brought in as an adviser, though the partnership did not last long. He cherishes his independence and the freedom to be outspoken.

'If there's a small accident on Amtrak, there are pictures of the wreckage on the front page of the *New York Times*. Back on page twenty-four you'll find a small item two inches high reporting that 50,000 people were killed on the highways in 1978. Right! Don't get on the safe old trains, get on the safe old highways and get yourself killed. Two million, three hundred thousand hospitalised in one year!'

Over the apple pie I asked Rogers what it had been like, riding the great trains such as the Twentieth Century and the Super Chief. Did romances spring up? He paused, then smiled and said, 'I regard that as a terribly personal question'. Another pause and a broader smile. 'Yes, in a word. As far as I'm concerned, twice.' A clearing of the throat and a third pause. 'Not bad either, as I recall. I hope there aren't any more questions like that.'

We drank a toast to the railroad in Mr Pins's claret. Then it was bedtime. I slept in one of the smaller bedrooms beneath a blanket, as in the old days. The lack of sheets and the noise of passing freight trains made for a restless night.

DAY TWO

In the daylight Harrisburg station looked as if it had been a major target in a recent air-raid. Half the roof was missing so that the rain poured through on to the tracks, the paint on the passageway walls was chipped and peeling, and apart from one or two vagrants the place seemed deserted. All this was a far cry from what the *Harrisburg Times* wrote in 1906, just two years after the present station buildings were completed.

There is no town in Pennsylvania that is so advantageously situated with regard to railroad connections as Harrisburg. From every point of the compass these great public thoroughfares of travel and trade enter the borough, and passenger and freight trains arrive and depart almost every hour. It is a scene of constant bustle and activity.

Rogers, never happy unless on the move, spent the day travelling in Harrisburg's only local train, to Philadelphia and back. In the evening the two sections of the Broadway Limited came in from New York and Washington, and when they had joined up, we said good-bye to Rogers and Mr Pins and the *Pennsylvania*, and climbed aboard. It was already dark as we headed towards the Alleghenies, so we didn't see the Rakisla bridge across the Susquehanna or the famous horseshoe curve at Altoona or the engine works at Lima. Instead we drank Budweiser in the club car and joined in a sing-song with some teachers who were trained in sign language for the deaf and dumb, and were on their way to a convention. Horace, the black barman, who had seen even longer years of service than the club car itself, kept the bar open until two.

The cocktail lounge on the Super Chief

DAY THREE

By dawn we had crossed the Alleghenies and were speeding through eastern Illinois. At breakfast came the unsurprising news that we were running two hours late. One of the camera crew organised a sweepstake on our time of arrival and I took the high field. We passed derelict Gary, the first of the white-painted houses of the Chicago suburbs, then came a glimpse of the city itself, and the first sights of whose soaring buildings takes the breath away. At eleven minutes past eleven we rolled into Union Station, which made me the winner of the sweepstake and richer by eight dollars. This was the end of the line for the Broadway Limited. We would stay the night in Chicago and the next evening put our things aboard the San Francisco Zephyr.

Chicago is still the pivotal city of America, the place where all lines meet. Forty thousand freight trains come in and out of here each day, shifting twenty million tons of goods a year. And not so long ago Chicago was the starting-point for one of the most famous of all North American luxury trains, the Atchison, Topeka and Santa Fe's Super Chief. This train used to carry just sixty passengers a trip along the Santa Fe's tracks between Chicago and Los Angeles. For a surcharge of ten dollars you got a barber's shop, a ladies' maid, valeting and a library; the women were given corsages and the men gold-edged wallets when they crossed the Californian border; it was a train for film stars and vice-presidents and other stinking rich.

At the Santa Fe's offices near the waterfront Fred Peterson, the former Head of Passenger Services, spoke about the Super Chief's standards:

The food had to be prepared perfect. You would see the supervisor's arm go up and stop the waiter. 'Take it back, put fresh parsley on it, that steak don't look too good, get a better one.' The waiters had to be just shiny. You had to be able to look at the brass buttons on their jackets and see yourself. If one of them should get a spot on his jacket, he would have to set down his tray, stop what he was doing and get a clean jacket immediately.

A waiter who once served on board the Super Chief recalled a European steward called Peter Lombardi.

Everything he would fix special for the celebrities would be 'à la Peter Lombardi'. I had a passenger ask once, 'Is the trout fresh?' Peter Lombardi said to her, 'Lady, I'll show you how fresh that trout is. Chef, take the trout out of the water and kill it for this lady!'

Another waiter remembered a trip when Clark Gable was aboard.

There was a vacant place next to him at the dinner table, so when this young girl came in – she couldn't have been more than about sixteen – I asked if he'd mind my putting her next to him. He said he'd be delighted, and he was as good as his word and gave her a great time. Next day I saw the girl writing a postcard. She showed it to me. It began, 'Mother, you'll never believe this, but last night I had dinner with Clark Gable.'

For those who could afford it the Super Chief (and to a lesser degree the Chief and the Captain) were the only means of getting to and from the west coast with speed and comfort. 'It was,' said Douglas Fairbanks junior, 'that bit faster, that bit more luxurious. It seemed very romantic somehow to go speeding through the wild west territory. At night you would hear this lonely hoot from the engine, and there was a great sense of the vastness all around one.'

DAY FOUR

The local paper told me they had recently run a photo-story of a man who had once taken snapshots of all the famous Hollywood stars as they arrived at Dearborn station from Los Angeles. His name was Len Liesewicz, and we arranged to meet him at Dearborn, or rather in the ruins that were once Dearborn, for the station was abandoned and left to rot years ago. The main building was still there, signs still pointed to the tracks, but there'd been no efforts made at either restoration or demolition. Len wandered around in the rubble and recalled his time there thirty years ago:

I was sixteen years old. My brother gave me this camera, and I started taking pictures. Nothing fancy. Just shoot. No flash. If the sun wasn't out, you were in trouble. One fifteen the train came in. Then the old waiting game.

In the forties and fifties security at railway stations was as tight as it is at airports today. Len Liesewicz was up against Hollywood agents, personal bodyguards, professional photographers. But he was a determined lad; and the Hollywood stars relented.

Laurel and Hardy, the Three Stooges, they posed for me. Then there was Dorothy Lamour, Joe Brown, Ralph Bellamy, Greer Garson, Hedy Lamarr – all big stars. They had state troopers protecting them but I got pictures. All to myself. Just a kid standing around in a jacket, asking actors and actresses to pose. All that stuff that happened then. And now nothing. It's a shame. I lost something that was a part of me. It was really terrific.

Over at Union Station, meanwhile, the deserted concourse began coming to life at around 4.30 p.m. as the first of the city's 250,000 evening commuters arrived to catch double-decker trains to suburbs like Harvey and Cicero and Skokie. An hour and half later, when the flood was once again dwindling to a trickle, I boarded the San Francisco Zephyr for the 2000-mile journey to the west coast. We would be following the old Union Pacific route, the first line ever to span the country.

After dinner (clear soup, salad with 1000 Island dressing, lamb cutlets, ice-cream) a man played popular songs on an old, upright, out-of-tune piano in the club car. One of them was 'Sentimental Journey'. Around midnight the sound of wheels changed to a lighter pitch and looking out of the window I saw water and lights and knew we were crossing the mighty Mississippi, for the early explorers the first great natural barrier to the west. Then, as I dropped off to sleep, I heard the train stop and knew it must be Omaha, now the headquarters of Strategic Air Command, but in 1865 the eastern terminus and starting-point of the Union Pacific Railroad.

An awakening in another world; the vast, golden, empty spaces of Nebraska, the heartland of America. During the night we had been running through the Platte River Valley which the Union Pacific's Chief Engineer, a young major-general named Grenville Dodge, had chosen as the route to the west. 'The Lord had so constructed the country,' he wrote, 'that any engineer who failed to take advantage of the great open road, would not have been fit to belong to the profession.'

Like many travellers since, Robert Louis Stevenson was overwhelmed by the vastness of the plains of Nebraska, an area as big as France:

We were at sea – there's no other adequate expression – on the plains of Nebraska. It was a world almost without feature, an empty sky, an empty earth. Front and back the line of railway stretched from horizon to horizon like a cue across a billiard board. On either hand the green plain ran till it touched the skirts of heaven. The train toiled over this infinity like a snail.

Had we been flying over this great green and golden sea, we would have seen nothing of it. Had we been driving across it, we would have become exhausted by it. But eating scrambled eggs and bacon and reading the paper as we crossed it by train was a marvellous experience; it was there to summon for our delight but it did not obtrude.

Others in America are also beginning to discover the joys of train travel; for in only nine years of operating Amtrak has increased its overall ridership by more than four million passengers a year. Two Louis Harris polls conducted in 1972 and 1978 showed increasing public interest in the railroads and a wish for more federal spending on the improvement of inter-city travel. If only Amtrak had appeared on the scene earlier and invested the kind of money in the railroads that British Rail did after the war, if only they had all-welded tracks everywhere and something equivalent to the British 125, what a joy intercontinental travel in America would be.

In English trains, on the whole, passengers try and avoid each other. But with breakfast over and three hours to fill in before reaching Denver, passengers on the Zephyr were eager to pass the time of day. They came in all sizes, from the purveyor of bromides ('The first time you meet someone on a train, they're kinda like a stranger to you, but after that they become your friend') to a young, dark-haired girl who had a real fear of flying. 'I don't care for planes. I don't trust anybody, especially some pilot I've never met. I feel physically uncomfortable in a plane. I don't much care for

train movements either, but planes are just intolerable.' She was also, it
turned out, an amateur astrologist. 'Each planet and constellation has a
different vibration. And they manifest in different conditions, and different
ways. Astrologers can certainly tell homicidal maniacs.'

Then there was a bearded youth who said to me: 'I'm going to Denver for
the ninth annual free university and learning network conference. I help
operate full circle resource exchange. This is what we call a learning
network, and the network is a telephone referral service.' I never did figure
out what he did.

And there was a granny, on her way to join her daughter in the west. 'I've
been on this train twice a year since 1951. I live out there now. I belong to a
group of over fifties, and everybody else in that group has moved out
because his or her children have moved out. That's the history of
California.'

At midday we rolled into Denver. I said good-bye to the grandmother
and astrologer and the man who was into full circle resource exchange.
And to the train. For I was going into the Rockies on a brief excursion and
would rejoin it in a couple of days' time.

DAY SIX

After the Mississippi, the Rockies were the next great natural barrier to
the building of a railroad to the west. Denver lies at their foot, which is
why it was not on the original Union Pacific line which runs clear of the
mountains to the north. But Colorado has a long history of railroading,
and the foothills of the Rockies are criss-crossed by the skeletons of tracks
built to meet the gold and silver booms at the end of the last century.

There are still one or two small-gauge private tracks in the area, but the
only standard-gauge railway still running through the Rockies is that of the
Denver and Rio Grande, the last long-distance passenger train in the United
States not owned by Amtrak. On three days a week its six coaches make the
thirteen-hour, 570-mile journey to Salt Lake City through some of the most
spectacular scenery in America; on the other three it returns. For much of
the way it follows the course of the Colorado River. In winter it takes
passengers to the skiing slopes of Vail and Waterpark, in summer to the
lakes and rivers around Glenwood Springs.

Not surprisingly the company loses money on its passenger services,
and when its ten ancient (but very comfortable) coaches wear out, it will
not have the resources to replace them. The company has asked Amtrak

either to take over the passenger service or to be allowed to close the line beyond Glenwood Springs (for very few passenger make the entire trip). But so far, because of the large profit the company makes on its freight trains, Amtrak has refused.

DAY SEVEN

An hour's drive into the Rockies and there are many relics of the railroad's once influential presence; tracks overgrown with vegetation, sleepers left to rot when the rails were taken away. Some of the old equipment, though, has been put to modern use. The wooden water tower, for instance, which used to stand sentinel at the eastern approach to the Moffat Tunnel, was recently dismantled, moved and re-erected a few miles away as a mountain greenery home.

A whistle toot away I visited another residence fashioned from old railway stock. One of the best-known and most enduring symbols of American railroading is the caboose, the guard's van which carried thousands of railwaymen to and fro across the country, and was their living-quarters for often weeks on end. Jim Keith, a bearded young easterner who came west in the early seventies, carted two cabooses eight thousand feet up into the Rockies and, having converted them into a home, laid the base for a profitable family business.

We were looking for an alternative life style, an alternative kind of house that we could afford. Our biggest problem was that people were used to the *Grapes of Wrath* kind of box-car with cars like this full of migrant workers. It was hard to convince people it was OK to do it, but luckily we started long enough ago to avoid restriction from the county.

I had the first caboose for experience and so Charlotte, my wife, and I were able to live up here with our boys throughout the summer when the weather was good enough. We hand-drilled our connections and hand-sawed just about everything. It was very aesthetic and it felt good to do our own house in this way. After three cars we found we had the equipment and know-how to continue doing it. So down here in our local town, we built a store out of several more train cars; now we sell train cars and deliver them anywhere.'

DAY EIGHT

Although Denver today is on the main line from Chicago to San Francisco, the original UP route ran through Cheyenne, a hundred miles to the north, and Denver had to be content with a branch line. In time the passenger route east of Cheyenne was closed, and then the Zephyr had to be taken in and out of Cheyenne from the junction on the main line at Borie, ten miles away.

Because of Cheyenne's legendary associations with Indians and cowboys, I decided to motor there from Denver, have a look round and catch the Zephyr when it came through in mid-afternoon. It was, as things turned out, a bad decision; for not only had it begun to snow when we left Denver and continued to snow all the way north, not only was Cheyenne as dull and bleak a place as any I've visited, but when we reached the Union Station, they told us that the Zephyr didn't run there any more. Only the day before it had come into Cheyenne for the last time; as from today passengers would be ferried by bus to join it (or leave it) at the halt at Borie.

In the waiting-room an old asthmatic gent who'd been a Zephyr passenger for years felt outraged.

'Why do they do it? It's not going to save them more than an hour. I've been riding this train for half a century. I think it's ridiculous.'

So a dozen of us climbed into a Greyhound bus and drove out to Borie. There wasn't anything to Borie but its name – though I did hear that Amtrak was thinking of building a waiting-room beside the track at a cost of three-quarters of a million dollars. It was snowing again at Borie so we stayed inside the bus while workmen hacked a path out of snow and ice to enable us to reach the train. When it finally showed up, it was an hour late.

Beyond Borie is the desert, 'mile upon mile of it', wrote Stevenson, 'and not a tree or a bird or a river. The train was the only piece of life in all the deadly land; the one actor, the one spectacle fit to be observed in this paralysis of man and nature.' And what was true in 1879 is just as true to-day.

The few towns along this stretch of the track – Laramie, Rawlins, Rock Springs – all owe their existence to the coming of the railroad ('roaring, impromptu cities,' Stevenson called them, 'full of gold and lust and death'). At one of them, Green River, I left the Zephyr to spend the night.

DAY NINE

Three years ago Green River and its adjacent town of Rock Springs recaptured something of their former lurid reputations when there was an unexpected mining boom, resulting in a desperate shortage of accommodation, large pay cheques, heavy drinking and whoring and a few impromptu murders. An American television network did a documentary –

which none of the inhabitants liked – about the town's wickedness. Today Green River and Rock Springs are respectable again, and almost as dull as Cheyenne.

Originally Green River was a staging-post on the overland, covered-wagon route to California. Then, in 1868, it became a railroad division station and an important junction; and from that time until recently its economy has been linked almost exclusively to the railroad. During the war freight traffic was such that there were queues of trains waiting to enter the station for up to thirty miles away. Even today, in a town with a population of only 4196, some 350 people still work for the railroad.

Green River was also immortalised by the Union Pacific's early official photographer, A J Russell, who took many pictures of the bridge there, with the town's famous landmark of Citadel Rock in the background. Russell went wherever the railroad labourers went, and his pictures of them grading, laying, blasting a track out of the wilderness, as well as relaxing in the shanty towns that became their temporary headquarters, provide a unique record of the building of the line west.

The labourers, mostly Irish, had much to contend with: poor food, primitive living conditions, little or no medical attention, and attacks by local Indians who feared the loss of their buffalo grazing-grounds. One of the worst of these was the Plum Creek massacre of 12 August 1867, when a band of Indians removed part of a bridge over a river-bed. This resulted in the derailment of a west-bound freight, and the deaths of the fireman and engineer. A passenger in the caboose managed to crawl to safety and alert the driver of the following train, though he was unable to prevent the Indians ambushing a telegraph repair crew. Before a platoon of soldiers arrived to drive the Indians away, three UP employees had been killed and two more were missing.

Yet despite temporary setbacks in the building of the line nothing could check the enthusiasm or sense of mission that had dominated the venture from the outset – so necessary to the healing of the country's wounds after the recent horrors and hatreds of the civil war. Thanks to General Dodge and his staff the building of the track was always ahead of schedule. By 1867 the line was 535 miles west of Omaha. In January 1869 milepost 1000 was erected in Weber Canyon, Utah, and soon became a big tourist attraction. Six years ahead of time the UP's tracks reached the flat plains north of Salt Lake City.

Today the Zephyr covers much of this journey in the dark. The 1000-mile

An emigrant train ticket for the Union
and Central Pacific Railroad Line of 1876–7

Union & Central Pacific Railroad Line.

Thos L. Kimball

Gen'l Ticket Agent, U. P. R. R.

8 4 2 4

ONE CONTINUOUS
EMIGRANT PASSAGE
—FROM—
OMAHA
TO STATION CANCELED.

Good for TEN DAYS only from and including date punched or indicated in the margin, after which time it will be "Void," and full fare will be charged for the whole or remainder of the trip, as the case may be.

Kelton.	Marysville.
Elko.	Terminus Oregon Division
Palisade.	Sacramento.
Battle Mountain	Stockton.
Winnemucca.	Lathrop.
Reno.	Terminus So. Pacific R.R.
Truckee.	San Jose.
Colfax.	San Franci .

NOT TRANSFERABLE.

No Stop-over privileges given on this Ticket.

Baggage Checked only to Destination.

Whole | 1876 | Half | 77

Dec. Nov. Oct. Sept. Aug. July. June. May. Apr. Mar. Feb. Jan.

17 1 19 3 20 4 21 5 22 6 23 7 24 8 25 9 26 10 27 11 28 12 29 13 30 14 31 15 16

3 10 31 1 25 1 2 27 7

marker has gone, though you can still see the site of Devil's Gate Bridge if you are prepared to dodge the traffic on the modern freeway that now dominates Echo Canyon. And, if you stand facing Citadel Rock at Green River, you can understand Russell's excitement as he staged his tableau to celebrate the achievement of those who had hacked four hundred miles of railroad track out of the desert in 1868.

DAY TEN

But while General Dodge and his Irish labourers were toiling across the plains from the east, another army of railroad builders – the Central Pacific's five thousand Chinese – were making their way from the west. Throughout the winter of 1868–9, they hacked and blasted a track through the snows and ice of the High Sierras – the last great natural barrier to the riches of California – and in the process built fifteen tunnels. At first the Central Pacific's managers were uncertain of how the Chinese would stand up to the work and the weather; but in the event they proved just as efficient and a good deal more sober than the Union Pacific's Irishmen.

In his efforts to push the CP's tracks as far east as possible before meeting those of the UP – for every mile of track laid brought an added government grant – the CP's Chief Engineer laid a wager of ten thousand dollars that his men would complete the laying of ten miles of track in one day. He won the bet. Such a feat has never been equalled anywhere in the world; and to-day in the middle of the desert in Northern Utah, a marker still commemorates the spot.

So greedy were the two companies for further riches that even when they had reached the same parallels they went on laying their tracks for miles past each other. Eventually a compromise was struck, and it was agreed that the two lines should officially be joined at Promontory, Utah, on 6 May 1869.

Today the main line goes through Ogden, forty miles to the south, and Promontory, still the same desolate scrubland as when the lines were first built, has become a national park. The state authorities have put down a couple of miles of track and built replicas of the two engines – the CP's Jupiter and the UP's No. 119 – that faced each other on the day the lines were joined. And on every anniversary, as well as special occasions like our visit, people from the nearby towns of Corinne and Brigham City and Ogden dress up as the chief participants and re-enact the ceremony of the Golden Spike.

The marker in the desert of Northern Utah which commemorates the 10 miles of track laid in one day

'We are met today,' declared a young schoolteacher dressed as the President of the Union Pacific, 'to commemorate the completion of a project which is a remarkable example of the vision, the determination and the labour of thousands of men in a Union which may be consummated for ever.'

'We are assembled here,' he went on, 'to complete a new and shorter route between Europe and the Orient, and to join the riches of the American west with the finished products of our industrial east. The brains, the sweat and the muscle of thousands of men joined in this great venture under the guidance of Almighty God.'

For the benefit of our cameras the Jupiter and the 119 chugged up and down the track, the townspeople threw their hats in the air, the Golden Spike was rammed home a dozen times. By mid-afternoon it was becoming chilly, the children were getting tired and it was time to return to Ogden. But in the re-enactment of this ceremony, one realised what an impact the joining of America must have had. Henceforth it was to be an integral part, not only of the country's travel and commerce, but of its folklore. Railroad prints, like those of Currier and Ives, reached a mass market, films were made of train robberies and crashes (in one early silent picture two engines were allowed to run headlong into one another) and John Ford's 'The Iron Horse' cost more to make than the railroad whose story it told.

That evening I discovered that Ogden's Union Station leads a double

East and West shake hands as the No. 119 faces the Jupiter in 1869

life. The main concourse is now the venue for Saturday-night dinner dances, and some delightfully tipsy Mormons there insisted on escorting me to the platform where the Zephyr was expected at midnight, to drink a toast to my (so help me) sixtieth birthday.

DAY ELEVEN

In the night we passed Reno and Elko and Winnemucca, crossed the Humboldt desert, and by dawn had reached Truckee in the foothills of the

The Zephyr enters the High Sierras after a fresh fall of snow

Sierras. The Zephyr crawled uphill towards the Donner Pass and soon we were among the pine-trees beside a tumbling river, above the snowline. This reminded Stevenson (as it did me) of our native Scotland. 'I am usually very calm over the displays of nature,' he wrote, 'but you will scarce believe how my heart leaped at this. I had come home, home from unsightly deserts to the green and habitable corners of the earth.' And a man from Maine, after suffering days of journeying across the arid desert, declared, 'By God, I smell pitch again!'

From the snows of the Sierras we came down to the sunshine of Sacramento, California's state capital. Here they've turned the original railroad station and adjacent tracks into a railway museum – probably the best in America. One of its prize exhibits is the private coach, *Gold Coast*, which has stained-glass windows, lace curtains and an antique fireplace with smoked glass above the mantel and was once the property of America's foremost railroad chronicler, Lucius Beebe. The day we visited, a ceremony was taking place to mark the museum's acceptance from the Santa Fe Railroad of Engine No. 1010, one of the nineteen that took the eccentric millionaire Death Valley Scottie and his wife on their record-breaking run in 1905 from Los Angeles to Chicago.

There were several hundred people there that day, mostly rail buffs with

an eye for the finer points of rolling stock, but what few of them realised was that one of the guides showing people round was a former professional hobo, UP Joe. UP Joe told me that although his hoboing days were pretty well over, occasionally he did take a weekend ride over the Sierras to try his luck at the tables in Reno. He said that some of the old-time hoboes had recently met up at a convention in Iowa. Hood River Blackie was there, also Frying Pan Jack and Steam Train Murray who, said Joe, was the undisputed King of the Hoboes. He showed me a picture of them together. They looked like Old Testament prophets.

After demonstrating how to jump on to a moving car without falling under the wheels, Joe said:

I was only ten, I guess, when I started. First time I didn't get far, maybe a couple of hundred miles. Then they grabbed me and sent me back home. I was a good boy for quite a while then, stayed home until I decided I got to go again and upped and took the first freight out of town. I ended up in Los Angeles, California. Took quite a while to get there, maybe three weeks, stopping here and there and seeing the sights. I really enjoyed it.

It wasn't too difficult. If a train was moving pretty slow, you could run alongside and jump in the box-car door. Most of the box-cars have plug doors now which means they're closed when they're running and so you can't get on.

The bulls, that's the railroad police, were very tough. How tough depended where you were. Southern California were pretty bad and one place in St Louis they'd even shoot at you. The Illinois Central had one where they all had nicknames. The one I especially remember was Winchester Pete of Carbondale, Illinois, because he'd shoot first and ask later. And Houston, Texas, was a bad place. If they caught you, they beat the hell out of you. And I mean work you over but good. By and large you didn't meet too many, but when you did, you'd better be moving.

DAY TWELVE

When the Central Pacific line was started, the railhead was at Sacramento; to reach San Francisco you took a river-boat. Today the Zephyr ends its journey anti-climactically at Oakland, across the water from San Francisco and not even in sight of the sea.

At Oakland we boarded the Coast Starlight, the most successful of all Amtrak's trains, which starts in the north at Seattle and runs down to Los Angeles. Art Lloyd, Amtrak's PR man on the west coast and who was also on the train, said its success was due to it serving every major college and university campus on the west coast. At holiday times like Thanksgiving

A hobo walking the tracks in the 1930s

and Christmas the Starlight carried a full load of 600 passengers; and this in a part of the country where the automobile and airplane are king. All the same, you have to have time to ride the Starlight. It's a lazy, ambling sort of train. The distance from Oakland to Los Angeles is about the same as from Edinburgh to London. That journey takes a little under five hours. This one took eleven.

Art Lloyd thinks that trains in the States are in for a comeback, and he may well be right. Anyone in a hurry and with a long way to go will always fly; but when it comes to a choice between automobile and train, there's little argument as to which is the least tiring and most fuel efficient. If the days of cheap and plentiful gasoline are now limited, as many Americans think, then the trains can only benefit. And on routes which are suffering heavy automobile and air traffic congestion such as the Los Angeles to San Diego run, Amtrak already is benefiting.

Amtrak's most pressing need is for new rolling stock and modernised tracks. On the east coast routes where Amtrak owns the permanent way and has brought new coaches and locomotives into service, the Metroliners that run between Boston–New York–Washington are now competitive with the airlines. It's the long-distance trains that are the worry. Most of the famous old named trains are now gone – the Empire-Builder which ran between Chicago and Seattle was taken off while we were over there – and the inauguration of others such as the Desert Wind, a luxury train travelling between Los Angeles, Las Vegas and Salt Lake City, are somehow an inadequate substitute. So long as Amtrak is the tenant and not the owner of the tracks it uses, its trains will never run as comfortably as they would wish and, with freight traffic always having priority, there can be no certainty about times of arrival.

The Starlight pottered southwards: there was time for a game of backgammon, a light lunch, a snooze. Then at Santa Barbara we hit the Pacific Ocean. 'On no other coast that I know,' wrote Stevenson when he saw it for the first time, 'shall you enjoy such a spectacle of ocean's greatness, such beauty of changing colour and such a degree of thunder in the sound.'

In the warm, early evening, we came into Los Angeles' Union Station. We had reached journey's end, we had travelled hopefully, laboured and arrived. It had been a great trip. If I'd gone by air, I'd have saved much time, of that there can be no doubt. But what would I have done with the time I would have saved?

Edna St Vincent Millay said it all:

> My heart is warm with the friends I make,
> And better friends I'll not be knowing,
> But there isn't a train I wouldn't take,
> No matter where it's going.

SOUTH AMERICA

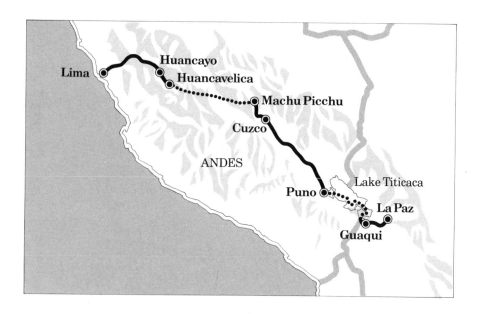

Three Miles High

MILES KINGTON

'To the station,' I said.

There was no need to tell the taxi driver which station. There is only one railway station in Lima, the so-called Los Desemparados station which is sited magnificently by the back garden of the Presidential Palace, bang in the centre of Lima. It is as if Euston were at 11 Downing Street.

'Ah, so you are taking the train,' he concluded. It was a fair conclusion; at 7.20 a.m., when nobody much else is stirring in Lima, it seems a fair bet that anyone hurrying in the direction of the President's Palace is either bent on a *coup d'état* or due to catch the 7.40 train. It was however a wrong conclusion.

'No,' I said. 'I just want to see the train leave, and have a look at the station.'

He turned round in his seat and looked at me.

'You want to *look* at the *station*?'

'Yes.'

'Señor, there are many more interesting things in Lima. I will take you on a tour.'

'No, thank you.'

'There are good museums here. There are old houses. We have many ruins. I do not think it is worth going to the station.'

Ah, but it is always worth going to the station. When I am landed in a foreign city I tend to make for the station just as other people feel impelled to do the cathedral or the big shops. Quite apart from the fact that the station is liable to be architecturally as impressive as anywhere else (Grand Central Station is still one of the finest cathedrals in New York), there is an excitement and mystery about a mainline station, especially a terminus, which are hard to rival. The lines snake out from the platform into the sunlight beyond and vanish for any of a thousand destinations. The people milling around could be on the verge of a long journey which will never bring them back, or about to take the same ten-mile journey which they take every day. The old Blackfriars Station façade used to have a list of its destinations carved in stone: down one side were inscribed the names of Sevenoaks, Bromley and other homely towns, while down the other in equal weight were announced Budapest, Istanbul, Cairo and all points beyond. I do not think one can ask for a single to Istanbul now, but the effect is still the same for me. Slightly magic.

I found this impossible to explain in my low-level Spanish, however.

'To the station,' I said.

He gave in silently. One should always humour madmen.

By 7.30 the station was already bustling with passengers and street salesmen – the two are inseparable in Peru. Doughnuts, sticks of bread, biscuits, curiously knotted bits of pastry, newspapers, cigarettes – anything designed to take you through a long journey – was on sale outside the grand ice-cream façade of Los Desemparados, though most of the arrivals seemed to be well equipped already, if not with snacks for the train, then at least with all their worldly possessions tied up in bundles. If they were Peruvians, they were mostly encumbered with large shapeless packages wrapped up in blankets; if young European travellers, they had those huge orange, aluminium-framed backpacks, with ancillary bedding rolls and surplus equipment attached like limpets, which are as much an ethnic part of their culture as the multi-coloured blankets are of Peruvian life. Into a dark hall they all poured, with stained-glass windows glowing grandly above them, then down a narrow staircase into the much less grand but more business-like waiting room, and the queue.

Ah, Peruvian queues! How patient they are, and how orderly. We English pride ourselves on our civilised approach to queuing, but the Peruvians can show us a thing or two. I had imagined that the Latin American temperament would make queuing a matter of competitive pride, but I had not reckoned with the place that bureaucracy has in their lives nor with the Indian tradition of long-suffering stolidity. That one lone ticket seller should have to cope with the hundreds hoping to board the train; that he should not seem to accelerate as departure time grew near; that the end of the queue would undoubtedly miss the train; none of this seemed to strike them as unfair, but simply as part of life's unrich pattern. One queue I did see in up-country Huancavelica where, five minutes before the train was due to go, those at the back panicked and rushed foward. A deep chant of 'Cola! Cola!' (Queue, queue!) broke out from those who thought they had a better than even chance of making it, and the interlopers slunk shamefaced back to their hopeless position.

At 7.40 precisely a bell rang, the ticket collector swung the heavy metal gates and shut and locked them, and together with the disappointed portion of the queue I watched the train slowly slide out of sight. Five minutes later the station was totally deserted, the ticket office closed and the station dog fast asleep in the middle of the tracks. He was in little danger there, for the last train of the day had just left. Not so long ago there used to be two trains a day, the ordinary train and the express train, but the difference between them was never more than between twenty and thirty miles per hour, their respective top speeds, and now there is just the one train a day leaving from the one platform in Lima's grand central station.

That a capital city should be served by no more than one daily train seems extraordinary to us, but it makes sense in Peruvian terms. For one thing, it is buses and not trains that are the true backbone of the transport system, and the ribs as well. For another, the train from Lima to Huancayo takes eight hours, but along the new road which shadows it all the way it is only five by car. And above all there is the fact that the railway was not really built for people. It was built to open up the interior and bring the mineral wealth of the Andes down to the coast.

Lima is a seaside town, standing in the strip of desert which runs almost all the way down the west side of South America, separating the Andes from the sea. It would be easy enough to build railways down through that flat featureless strip, joining the town and ports that tend to occur where a river mouth has created a settlement, from Ecuador through Peru and deep into Chile. But a hundred years ago, in the great days of railway building, that need was already satisfied, if not by roads, then by sea transport which was well developed and able to jump the problems caused by national frontiers. No, what was needed was a thrust into the interior, to the mines placed infuriatingly on top of the Andes, to the great silver mines up in Bolivia, to the ore deposits inside Chile. That is why a railway map of South America shows so many lines at right angles to the sea, running away from the main centres and never connecting up with the next line down the map. The energy of the great railway-makers went into driving railroads into places where there were not even roads, only mountain paths.

'To the station,' I told the taxi driver.

'You saw the station yesterday,' he said. 'Today let me show you some ruins.'

'Today I am catching the train.'

That was why I got up at 6.00 and arrived at the station at 6.30. Once you have gained respect for a Peruvian queue, you like to be somewhere near the head of it. But I had not made allowances for another Peruvian habit, that of being late for most things, and the station was not yet unlocked. I retired across the road to a small restaurant oddly called El Lunch Café and had a cup of coffee. Nothing more. I had been told very strictly that the first time you hit altitude, there is nothing like a full stomach to bring on nausea. My eyes, roving round the lunch café, lit on a large mirror presented by Andrews Liver Salts. 'Sal de Andrews,' it said; 'Lista al Instante'. Buy your liver salts now, seemed to be the message, because by God you're going to need them at the top. I ignored it.

So, leaving the friendly surrounds of the Lunch Café, full of familiar products such as Te Horniman and Scotch Whisky (made by distilleries one never hears of in Britain but which seem to export direct to dusty cafés in Graham Greeneland), I again crossed to the station, descended into the bowels and became a member of the queue in my own right.

What I haven't mentioned so far is that I was also very nervous.

Travel writers never mention this.

But going to Peru was, for me, rather like meeting a very famous film star or a member of the Royal Family for the first time. However blasé you are outwardly, even cynical, inwardly there is just one thought on your mind: not to make a fool of yourself. I know in my heart of hearts that if I got into the same lift as Greta Garbo, I would ask her very casually which floor she wanted, lean forward to the control panel and press the alarm bell by mistake. Peru has many film star qualities. It not only has the highest railway in the world – which is why I was there – but the charismatic Andes, the Inca city of Cuzco, the legendary forgotten city of Machu Picchu, the llama and the highest working lake in the world, Lake Titicaca. I was due to meet them all. Would my table manners be good enough to meet this all-star cast?

My only advantage was that I had started in Lima, which it is hard to be overawed by. It has faded charm, but it isn't exciting, like a raddled film-star whose name you know but none of whose films you can remember. Residents of Lima tend to apologise for their city, saying that when they first arrived there it still bore marks of grandeur, most of which have been pulled down in order to make way for anonymous pieces of international architecture or building sites. The trouble is that however far you go back you never seem to arrive at Lima's great period. Charles Darwin arrived here over a hundred years ago in the *Beagle* and noted then that it must once have been a very fine city. I doubt it. I think it has always been a faded film star.

The Andes, however, are different, and I could tell that everyone fore and aft of me in the queue was on good talking terms with the Andes, and that only I had sweating palms at the thought of our first meeting. The unshaven policeman; the little old ladies bent under their blanket-loads, who might only have been thirty; the young workmen; the young wife who seemed to be saying a tearful goodbye to her husband though he later turned up on the train with her; the nun; the Identikit-bag Europeans with their curly beards if male and strong straight chins if not – there was not a single qualm among them at the thought that in four or five hours we would be going higher than railway passengers had ever gone before. It didn't matter; I carried enough social terror for the whole queue.

The train was divided into first and second class, both of reasonable quality and both remarkably cheap – even the first-class passengers were charged barely one pound or two dollars for an eight-hour journey – but, as if obeying some unspoken travel book rule, the more Indian-looking passengers crammed themselves into second class and I, together with most of the Europeans and any Peruvian above workingman level, found myself

An Andes-class steam locomotive at Lima

in first class. A shiny padded seat. A table. Plenty of stout metal luggage racks. Not so unlike England, which was in fact where the coaches had been made. I positioned myself with my back to the engine. Everyone I had talked to had been most insistent on this, when they had not been insistent about eating nothing on the journey, because when I came to the best bit of the journey I would find myself facing forward. I did not understand the reasoning behind this, but looked forward to finding out.

From where I sat I could see in the unfashionable part of town, away from the President's Palace, an enormous hill, conical, brown and empty, except for a huge cross at the top and below it an even huger political slogan: VOTE APRA. I did not understand the presence of the hill either. Lima was set in a flat strip of desert separating the Andes from the sea. What was this huge hill doing here already, looking even bigger and closer than Arthur's Seat in Edinburgh?

Scraping my Spanish together, I asked the Peruvian opposite if this was the first example of the Andes to be seen. He smiled pitifully at my ignorance.

'That is the Cerro San Cristobal. It is just a tiny . . .' he gestured with his

fingers to conjure up the Peruvian concept of a pimple '. . . it is nothing.' I
had made my first social gaffe with the Andes. 'People sometimes walk to
the top for a religious procession. Sometimes they walk to the top for a
political demonstration. It is very convenient – you can get up and down
before lunch.'

And what was APRA?

'That is our workers' party. You know we are having an election? It is the
first election since, oh, since the mid-sixties. Ever since then we have had
generals in power, but now they are calling for a civilian election.'

An orderly return to democracy?

'Perhaps. I think the generals are just tired of trying to run Peru, or
maybe they have all made their fortune and are now getting out. Everyone
is very tired of the generals, I know that. So now we have three big
candidates for the next president. There is the APRA man, Armando, who is
very popular. There is Belaunde, who was president in the 60s and was
thrown out by the generals, in fact he was put on to an aeroplane wearing
only his pyjamas, you know that story? He is still popular. And there is
Bedoya, who has been mayor of Lima and was responsible for building our
big expressway in the city and is of course very popular as Peruvians like
driving fast.'

And who will win?

'Ah, that is the question. Armando is perhaps the least likely, as a return
to left-wing politics would perhaps tempt the generals to come back again.
So I think maybe it will be Belaunde. A vote for the man thrown out by the
generals is a vote against the generals, you see? But it will not make much
difference whoever comes in.'

A bell rang. People ran to the train. The ticket collector glanced at the
clock, which was made in London, England, let the last passenger through
and locked his gates. Through the bars I could see the resigned faces of
tomorrow's queue. And then with a hoot the orange diesel engine jerked
the train alive; the Peruvian businessman opposite me opened his paper;
the station dog ran along snapping at the heels of the train; and we were
off.

The outskirts of Lima are as boring as any outskirts, but even boredom can
have its own flavour if you're not used to cactus plants and brown mud
walls, sub-Spanish churches and Raymond Chandler-vintage American
cars. The graffiti on the mud walls were endlessly varied. Not in the

Indians sell food and trinkets alongside the railway line

messages, which were all promises of victory and progress in the elections to come, pledges to smash this and undertakings to unite that, but in the initials of the parties making the pledges. There must be dozens of parties contesting the elections, and all are incomprehensible. (In Bolivia, later, I found a party whose initials were PUB, though it turned out to be not a Real Ale movement but the United Party of Bolivia.) The businessman confirmed that they were all real parties, but some had not been around for years; the more faded graffiti had been there since the last election fifteen years ago.

The line out of Lima runs alongside the main road into the hills; buses, cars and lorries have little trouble overtaking the train which never goes much over 30 mph. Yet even at that speed the train hoots much of the time, a mournful echoing hoot, which seemed to contain more than one note in it though I could never make out if this was because it was a genuine chord or just one strong note with overtones. It hoots because of pedestrians. The Peruvians tend to use the railway line as a private pathway, even to drive their animals along, and at each suspicious bend, or small settlement, or possible crossing, the driver hoots. In the early days of the railway a great many Indians and llamas were killed; nowadays casualties are low and mostly confined to animals who die near the line and are dragged to a position where a court might conceivably hold the railway company guilty.

On your right (as the guide book might say) note the occasional small village, green and flowery, at one of which we stop to pick up schoolchildren who leave at the next stop. On your left, if you are quick, spot a vast ramp leading up to a bridge that was never built. It was to have led to the home of General Velasco, the man who led Peru from the sixties to the seventies, but who was ousted in 1975 before the bridge was finished, and died shortly after. While I was in Peru there was an attempt to blow up his tomb; the Peruvians may take time to get round to things but even by their standards this is an absurdly late assassination plot. On both sides notice amazingly fertile fields, fed by the River Rimac, and beyond them see the brown hills getting bigger and getting closer, squashing the fields nearer and nearer to the middle.

And a few miles ahead of us make a note of Chosica, where the wealthier Lima people (or Limeños) go for the sunshine. A curious thing, this; for much of the year seaside Lima is hidden in a grey blanket of cloud coming off the cold Humboldt current, and you have to go fifteen miles inland to rise above it. Not that it rains in Lima; the last time that that grey cloud provided more than a Scotch mist was in 1971, or 1927, or 1919, depending on which Limeño you believe. Lima depends entirely for its water supply on the poor old Rio Rimac, which as a result reaches the sea as a tiny trickle, when it should be its proudest moment.

But today is one of those rare May days when the sun still shines in Lima and, although I am cheated of the moment when we burst out of the mist at Chosica, it means that I can go and sit on the train steps. I get restless in trains, always convinced that unless I move about the whole time, I am going to miss something sensational or significant, and that unless I stick my head out of the window I shall see nothing. British Rail does not cater for people like me. Trains go faster and faster, making it harder and harder to put your head out of a window without getting it knocked off or your ears blown inside out, and now that we have finally been forced to sit tidily in our seats, it is smoking the windows so that we seem to be looking, not at the countryside, but at an old and faded print of the countryside. The Peruvian railways – Enafer Peru, they are called – are much more enlightened. They provide doors which you can open, steps you can sit on, and a speed which will not shake you off. The curious thing is that by one of the little-known subsections of the Law of Relativity Peruvian trains seem that much faster than British Rail Inter-City; sit outside in the sunshine with the wind whipping in at you, and the mournful hoot flying past you in tatters, and you feel carried along at a fair old rate, whereas inside the smooth smoked observation box of the London-Manchester express you hardly seem to be moving at all.

Chosica comes and goes. Having regained my seat for fear of having it taken by a Chosica person (a Chosiqueño?), I watch the waiter wiping the tables free of all the dust which has flown in the windows since Lima and taking orders for breakfast. I risk another coffee. From inside his newspaper the businessman orders eggs and bacon and fried potatoes, I think. I go back to my outdoor seat not wishing to miss San Bartolomé, where the mystery of facing backward and forward will be cleared up.

It was quite simply, really. Just half a zigzag.

When Henry Meiggs (about whom more later) built this railway in the 1860s and 1870s, he realised early on that he could not go straight to the top. The grade from Lima to the lowest possible top point was something like 6%. The maximum gradient he could build was 4%. Anything steeper and the trains would roll backwards. This is what is known technically as an insoluble problem. But the Victorians had a knack of dealing with such problems, or rather of not admitting defeat, and Meiggs soon decided to use zigzags or switchbacks. He would build a line as far as it would go and then, when faced with a blank mountain wall or cliff edge, would have the line go backwards towards Lima *but still climbing*. After a few hundred yards the line would go forward again and soon pass many feet above the same blank wall or cliff, having created a huge Z in the line to gain height. There was never much room at the end of those zigs and zags, and sometimes they were built out on wooden trestles above the void; sometimes trains had to change direction half at a time, which lost hours of running time overall. But it had to be done, and it was done thanks to the boundless energy of Henry Meiggs.

At San Bartolomé there is only a zig, or perhaps a zag. The train runs into the station. The engine comes off the front, turns on a turntable, fixes itself to the other end of the train and goes off in an enormous arc round the next hill, ending up facing the Andes again, which I was too by this time. Not, though, before I had had my first taste at San Bartolomé of Peruvian wayside snacks.

It is very hard to be enthusiastic about food in a place like Peru without arousing the hatred of the third world lobby. They cry, don't you know about malnutrition and starvation in Latin America? How can you praise the food when there are children starving in the streets? Quite so. I admit this. Having said which, I must say that a) I saw no children starving in the streets; b) Peruvian food can be terrific, especially the wayside snacks. In the towns they are more ambitious; a small stall on wheels will contain a tiny burner on which they will do you a local doughnut, a fried egg roll, a meat pie, hot pastry, anticucho (sort of kebab made of heart and potato), tamales (stuffed maize roll) or, best of all, chicharrones, bits of pork meat fried in their own fat.

San Bartolomé was simpler, more health food-based, offering only plain bread or fruit. But what fruit! Things I had never seen before, or only read about, paw paws, guavas, huge avocados and something called maracuya. I bought one in defiance of my diet. It was large, green, slightly sour and totally refreshing. The businessman nodded. Yes, he never personally ate them but there was a new canning factory which turned out very good tins of maracuya juice. He seemed prouder of the factory than the fruit.

It was now sunshine all the way. The hills were immense on either side though drier and browner than any we are used to. Not as arid as those near Lima, which are more like gigantic piles of builders' rubble and totally unused for cultivation. Still brown, though, and sporting only the scrubbiest vegetation, like a man who won't admit that his stubble will never become a beard. Sometimes the train ran high up on the hillsides itself, through short tunnels and over sudden bridges, but mostly clinging to footholds on the insecure-looking rock formations. Sometimes, usually before the next zigzag and another gain of height, it would return near to the valley bottom, and then there would be tiny fields, clusters of eucalyptus trees, wayside crosses, shacks and farms. Native women, too, mostly bent forward in a kind of fast shuffle-walk imposed on them by the weight of their loads, despite which they often contrived to be doing something else at the same time – feeding a child, knitting, sowing, reaping.

And inside the train I had also made contact with that other strange tribe, the backpackers, the European and American international hoboes, the graduate students doing their PhD on the rough side of the world. On other days in that train I was to find mostly Dutch, Germans and French, but today for some unknown reason they were almost all Scots and English. Mostly they were travelling in pairs, a few alone, with one quartet of Swiss girls. Although they did not say so in so many words, South America has now replaced the Himalayas as the magnet for the footloose young, with Peru playing the part of Nepal, and Cuzco standing in for Kathmandu. Yet in a curious way they did not seem to be excited by where they were. The first time I exclaimed at the sight of some Indian woman managing to knit, suckle and farm all at the same time, they turned wise but dry eyes on me.

'Ah yes,' they said, 'this is your first time out here. We have seen it all before in Ecuador and Colombia.'

And they returned to their non-stop talk of cheap hotels, most amazing rip-offs, worst hassles and best short cuts, without, it seemed to me, looking out of the window at what the *South American Handbook* calls 'views without compare'. The *Handbook*, a British guide completely revised each year, is accepted to be the best there is, yet even that is overtaken by time and accident, and our coach was nothing but a travelling seminar on gaps in the *Handbook*, with each group offering its own personal contributions based on personal experience.

Listening to them talk was impressive. I had never travelled rough like them nor will I now. I have not been to Sri Lanka, the Philippines, Australia, under my own power, working here and there to finance the next stage. I did not know that the places to go now are Easter Island and the Galapagos Islands. (Or were in 1980. I suspect the South American jungle is now the place.) I have not, like the four Swiss girls, been robbed by a purse-snatcher whom they then chased and beat the living daylights out of.

And yet, I don't know, there was something sad about their talk as well. Almost all of them were trained people – electronic engineers, teachers, mechanics, forestry graduates – and they had deliberately stepped aside from the capitalist, or at least business, world for a time, and yet because of their need to economise and find whatever was cheapest, they were more obsessed with money than a stockbroker. More than this, they seemed trapped on a roundabout which was becoming increasingly difficult to get off. Some of them had been travelling non-stop for three or four years and were secretly tired of it, yet driven to go on to places they hadn't yet seen even if their reflexes were numbed in advance.

'I'd actually quite like to get back to England and a job,' the mechanic confided in me. 'I'd find it hard now, though. The people I know have moved on and I haven't got the contacts, and of course jobs are becoming scarcer in Britain. I don't even know if I'm an up-to-date mechanic any more. I'll just have to keep travelling.'

Odd, too, that they were all about the same age, coming up to their thirtieth year. Ten years older than them, I've often wondered why I haven't been swept away and replaced by a new generation of journalists, and smarter younger people. Could it be, I now wonder, that they are a lost generation backpacking endlessly round the world, storing up marvellous experiences for books they will never get round to writing?

Henry Meiggs's tomb is in the posh graveyard in Lima. It's a rough block of granite, carved or just ripped out of the Andes, and looking even more boulder-like among the marble mausoleums surrounding it, containing the mortal remains of Peru's top families or men who were shot untimely before they could take over. It's a fitting grave. Meiggs was a dynamic, gritty American who left America after making and losing a couple of fortunes (his creditors are said to have chased his boat down the bay out of San Francisco and lost him in an opportune fog) and made his name by building a railroad in Chile. Ahead of time. Inside budget. Such a thing was unknown in South America, and the Peruvians decided that he was the man to build the railway they needed from Lima to the mines. He devoted the rest of his life, nearly twenty years, to forcing his way to the top of the Andes; though it finally broke him it's doubtful if without him a railway would ever have been built.

The time was right, as Peru was at the height of its guano boom. Guano a natural fertiliser in the shape of bird droppings, covered Peru's offshore islands, and what the birds had taken thousands of years to provide was mostly stripped in a decade of feverish fortune-making, feeding the fertiliser-hungry markets of Europe and America. The cash was there to build the railway and Meiggs was there to do it. As a work-force he used gangs brought with him from Chile, Chinese labour which had been tricked into coming to dig the guano and some ex-slaves of African descent. With the money granted him by a grateful nation, he bought the best equipment England could provide, though it often turned out not as good as the American equivalent. And with countless tons of explosive he started blasting his way towards the top of the Andes, whose mineral wealth was then brought painfully down by mule – he himself, in fact, was often forced to use mulepower to take the necessary equipment up – and in the process almost bankrupted Peru and certainly bankrupted himself.

Henry Meiggs, Don Enrique, they called him, was a charismatic but not, I would guess, a likeable man. His one biographer starts out with a terrific admiration of this swashbuckling American Pizarro, and ends almost distastefully listing the chicanery and bribery to which Meiggs stooped simply to continue the line. When he died the guano boom was over, the money had run out and the railway, though surveyed and part-engineered to the top, had only been built as far as Chicla. It lay dormant for some years till the bond-holders, all European, did a deal via London with the Peruvian government to finish the line if the profits remained in their hands. Thus was born the Peruvian Corporation, a British-based company which ran the railways until their nationalisation in the 1970s. The story of the Corporation is a good and exciting one (especially as told in *The Railways of the Andes* by Brian Fawcett, son of the famous Colonel Fawcett, and one of the top dogs in it for many years) but will always be overshadowed by the feats of Meiggs and his chief engineer Malinowski.

And yet, and yet. Whether it was because I had read too much beforehand, or because a finished piece of engineering conceals the struggle involved, or simply because it was a great and sunny day, I never felt as overawed on that ascent as I should have done. Perhaps I simply enjoyed it too much. As one zigzag followed another, as we rushed through tunnels between gorges, as we emerged from the dark on bridges high over the Rio Rimac (looking much healthier up here) and banged into the dark again, it suddenly seemed the most natural thing in the world to be hooting up through the Andes. In the middle of one vast valley, with the sky shut on both sides, and half the passengers fast asleep, the businessman finally told me that I could consider myself in the Andes now. But I felt I knew the lady already. Film stars, when you meet them, are just ordinary people inside the glamour. I'd forgotten that.

All this time the train had been climbing into thinner and thinner air, but to my great relief I found myself not affected by the height except for a certain shortness of breath – certainly not by any of the nausea or migraine that hits some people. Nobody seems to know why some are affected and some not. The only theory that occurs to me, somewhat wryly, is that as a smoker I am already used to oxygen deprivation. As it is unfashionable, not to say illegal, to suppose any advantages in smoking, I will not press the point. None of the backpackers seemed affected either (I suppose they had got used to it in Ecuador or Colombia), but one or two Peruvians fell back suddenly looking very pale and gasping for life, and for them there was a man with an oxygen tank, or rather a bag, which he held under one arm and dispensed like a very primitive set of bagpipes. The nozzle was stuffed into the patient's nose and he let them have two minutes' worth; they seemed a little happier afterwards. He offered me some as well; never one to turn down a free drink of any kind, I took a few deep sniffs and felt absolutely no difference whatsoever. But I was glad to have met what must, I suppose, be the only example of a medical attendant working full-time on a train.

Most of the results of altitude are not to do with the lack of oxygen but with the loss of pressure which results in, among other things, the boiling point of liquids being progressively lower. At 15,000 feet it takes nearly ten minutes to boil an egg. (At over 50,000 feet, your blood boils – worth remembering if you go ballooning.) A bottle of beer, bottled at sea-level pressure, froths over your trousers when you open it. And for the same sort of reason, man seems more prone to wind. I offer this in a spirit of scientific observation.

I now come to a matter of some delicacy. While the frailer among us had been quaffing oxygen, the train had left the gorges and cliffs behind and come out into the upland at nearly 16,000 feet. Although there were crags and peaks round us, one of them being Mount Meiggs topped by a stiff metal flag of the type later used on the moon, the train itself was running peacefully through grassy flatlands past a still and forbidding-looking lake, towards the top point of all. But it is not strictly speaking the highest piece of railway in the world. There is a branch line round the mountain to a mine, which is higher, but only carries freight. There is a siding here which goes higher. There is even in Bolivia a small line with some claims to being higher. But what this is beyond any doubt is the *highest regular passenger line in the world*. That seems satisfactory.

Or would do, were it not that the highest point itself is inside the longest tunnel on the line. There is something rather anti-climactic about celebrating such a record in the dark – it is rather like insisting on climbing Everest only at night – and so the Peruvian authorities have wisely placed all the triumphant altitude claims on a notice board well clear of the tunnel. When I came to script the film for which I was here I wanted to have a short sequence in the dark with triumphant music in the background and a voice saying: 'This is colour television's darkest hour', but they thought not. Wisely, too, I think.

The most extraordinary thing about the tunnel is that it lies on the watershed of the Andes. A river rising at one end would flow down to Lima, 100 miles away – at the other, it would flow east in the opposite direction, join the Amazon after many days and finally flow out to sea thousands of miles distant. This, relates Fawcett, was once vouchsafed to an American VIP who was on a courtesy trip up the railway. The VIP demanded that his train be stopped in the middle of the Galera Tunnel and although somewhat surprised the train crew did what he asked. He left the train, strode into the dark and returned a minute later, buttoning his trousers up. 'There!' he cried. 'I have achieved a great ambition. I have watered the Atlantic and Pacific oceans simultaneously.'

This story never quite made it to the film either.

Over the top and out of the tunnel, I had a very strong feeling (apart from that of hunger) that I was suddenly on familiar territory. The terrain had changed absolutely. No more of the craggy, skyscraping mountains on either side, but instead rolling, softer country. Sheep country, perhaps. Then it clicked. It was very like parts of Scotland, even if on a grander scale. Whereas the ascent had been through country the like of which I had never seen, this was landscape I could understand. What I couldn't quite understand was what it was doing at 16,000 feet, which is unusually high for parts of Scotland. But then, however often I made that train journey, I would never quite comprehend how one could be higher than Mont Blanc in a train.

From now on we were descending. We had passed the train going the other way. We were more than halfway there and there was a feeling of arrival rather than departure, even though there were still several hours to go. It may be because of this that I had a change of heart towards the backpackers; more probably it was because I had felt that they formed a society in which I had no place, and to which I could offer nothing. That all changed abruptly. They realised that I would soon be going back to

England and could carry messages. One group wanted films taken back
and sent to parents in Glasgow. Another lad, whose mother in King's Lynn
was worried about him, wondered if I could possibly drop her a note
saying he was looking well. 'She'd be impressed if a man from the BBC said
that. She might stop worrying.' Man from the BBC? Hmm. Well, just for
this once, in a good cause, I would agree to be called such. But above all
they wanted to know football results. How were Everton doing? And
Nottingham Forest? And who was in the Cup Final? I knew nothing about
cheap hotels in South America, but just for a moment – and thank God I
kept up with the soccer results – I was a mine of useful information.

Down and down through Scottish hills we went till we came to a town
which I hope exists nowhere in Scotland – La Oroya makes Glasgow look
like Oxford. It is the centre of the Peruvian mining industry and is a dark,
dirty, smoky, sprawling, litter-laden, polluted, unhappy town, whose one
claim to fame is the highest chimney in the world. Quite how ghastly it is
you do not realise till you pass through it by road and see the backside of the
miners' settlements – barracks, almost – which come down to the banks of
the River Mantaro, and are separated from the water by the most
grotesque chutes of rubbish I have ever seen. Water, did I say? Chemically
the Mantaro cannot be classified as water, only as effluent. God help the
people who have to work in this cheerless place. The slogans on the back of
their stark dwellings had no truck with the initials of the Peruvian parties
– they called directly on Marx and Mao to help them, and perhaps they
seem a slightly brighter prospect than God. I know that if I were a worker
at La Oroya I would find voting for David Steel, which I dimly remembered
doing at the last election, somewhat irrelevant.

After La Oroya, however, it was back to the Scottish lowlands (good old
David Steel) which gradually opened out into one of the most magnificent
valleys I have ever seen. Wide and fertile, with maize and bullocks and
eucalyptus growing everywhere, and distant hills grandly enclosing the
horizon, and even a thunderstorm growling to itself ten miles away (what a
landscape it must be that has room for a thunderstorm while elsewhere
business is continued as normal in bright sunshine), it opened the mind out
as far as it could go.

It was here that I finally got round to asking the Peruvian businessman
what his business was and finding that he was not a businessman at all, but

a meteorologist at Lima airport, going to join his wife on holiday so that they could enjoy the mountains together. In this he was an oddity – not in enjoying the mountains, I mean, but in going by train, because I now realised if I had not realised it before that train travel to a smart Lima inhabitant is rather unsmart. Rather like taking a bus overnight from London to Edinburgh. He was the nearest there was on the train to a professional person and he knew, he said, that it was odd to find him there but he revelled in it. He was the only Peruvian I met who enjoyed travelling on trains for their own sake.

The sun was now low in the sky and casting the most enormous shadows in each eucalyptus grove we passed through, as well as creating a golden dusty haze around the train. I had retreated again to the steps by this time, sitting in open air as potent as champagne, simply content to watch the amazing valley slip by. Looking backwards was like looking along one of those endless French roads punctuated by perfectly placed tall trees (occasionally boys would run out of the woods as we passed to put their ears on the line and listen to the retreating vibrations). Looking sideways was like watching a prizewinning film on rural life in South America. For some reason my eye was especially caught by one woman in the fields, trudging homewards after a hard day in my very own documentary, with a small bullock in front of her and a smaller child behind her. What possible connection, I thought, could there be between her routine earth-bound life and my privileged ever-changing existence? It was as if I were producing and directing her, and she not knowing a thing about it, me being a god-like creature and her being condemned every day to return to her rut. Hubris, indeed.

It was about a minute after that that the train came to a halt on a bridge. In Britain that would be no cause for alarm. A train ahead, perhaps. A signal. But in Peru there are no trains ahead, or behind, and precious few signals, and there can be only one reason for an unexplained halt: a mechanical failure. We Europeans did not realise this and sat in our seats for a short while, waiting for the train to go on; when it did not, we left the train and walked to the engine to see in a curious sort of way what was happening. The Indians on the train, wiser than us, knew instinctively that once stopped the train would not start again and one by one they gathered their belongings together and made for the main road visible in the trees half a mile away. The meteorologist said apologetically to me that he too felt it was time to leave the train, but that it was only twenty miles to Huancayo and he was sure we would all get there somehow. Before long the train was empty of Peruvians and full of Europeans.

The engine driver, meanwhile, was busy inside the works of his engine, looking as if any moment he would stumble across the missing link. I had every faith in him. I had only marginally less faith when he re-emerged from his examination and asked the small congregation if anyone had a knife on them. At the third time of asking I understood his Spanish and said yes, I had a penknife on me. I tossed it up to him. He looked at it quizzically, thought it might do and disappeared back inside the guts of the engine.

Now, if I had thought hard about the matter it should have occurred to me that an engine driver who borrows a penknife from one of the passengers is not the most likely person in the world to have everything under control, and yet so imbued was I with the European notion that daddy knows best that even then I stood patiently by waiting for the train to go again. But by this time the train was no longer a dominant part of the landscape, charging imperiously through all it surveyed. It had become vegetation. Another derelict machine in that part of the farmyard where derelict machines are laid to rest. Once immobile, it was simply an object round which rural life could flow. A farmer returning home with his small herd of animals (one bullock, one dog, one goat) proceeded under the railway bridge as usual, that is, with great difficulty, and the few remaining passengers set to with a will to help him beat the beasts on their homeward path. And then who should walk by but the selfsame woman in the fields on whom I had looked down in such lordly fashion. How changed our positions were! She looked at us with a faint passing interest, and perhaps even a touch of pity, and then went on home.

By the time the engine driver had admitted defeat and given me my penknife back, the train was almost empty. I picked up my heavy bags and set off for the road, fully conscious that at that altitude one shouldn't walk a long way with heavy bags but not knowing what else to do. The road was lined with refugees from the train, all thumbing lifts. If I had been a lorry driver going to Huancayo, I would certainly have given a lift to a single hitchhiker, but faced with groups of thirty or forty I think I would have driven on. I know these lorries did. So I walked to the next garage to see if there was a telephone I could use, though I was not sure who I was going to telephone. A taxi, perhaps?

There was no telephone in the village, said the garage man. Nor a taxi either. However, his brother did have a car, and perhaps for a small sum of money he might be persuaded to drive to Huancayo . . .

Huancayo, according to the tourist brochure, is a convenient centre for many interesting places nearby. That is inevitably another way of saying that there is nothing very interesting in Huancayo itself, and that is true enough. It's a large, sprawling market town with the usual ration of banks, churches and bus depot. There had also been till recently a large dance hall but it was now closed down on safety grounds. Why, oh why, wailed the leader in the local paper, are things always the same in Peru? Why do we adopt temporary measures which are then taken as a permanent solution?

I expect the same has been said of the railway line which goes on from Huancayo. It was built by the Peruvians themselves, the only line in Peru of which this can be said, and for economy reasons it is narrow gauge. They would like to have converted it to diesel engines, but can only afford to have replaced half their steam engines – one old American-built Baldwin dates from 1920, the year the line was opened. They would like, above all, to have built the line as far as Ayacucho, the next big town down the Andes, instead of which it goes to Huancavelica, a mercury-mining town in the back of beyond, and then peters out. It is given only fleeting mentions in guide books.

And yet almost as soon as the train started the next day, I knew that this was the railway line I had come to see. Partly, I suppose, because I was now the only European on the train, and I felt I was deep into Indian territory at last, totally surrounded by dark faces. Partly because the hills on either side of the valley were covered in cultivated terraces reaching as high as the eye could see, remnants of the old Inca farming system. But above all because this line was not just, as the Lima-Huancayo line was, simply a means of getting somewhere; it was also a lifeline to the country we passed through. At every station people greeted relatives, collected long-awaited bundles, welcomed sorely needed supplies, got on with livestock for market, or climbed aboard to sell their produce to the passengers, not bothering to get off till the next station. One coach was almost entirely filled with a band of musicians going up to Huancavelica to play at a fiesta that night, at one of the mines. I saw the most Inca-looking of them wake from a deep sleep and get up to remove from the luggage rack a case containing, of all things, a tenor saxophone. From the case he took a

A steam engine on the Huancayo–Huancavelica line which runs at 10,000 feet above
sea level

carefully wrapped bottle and settled back into his seat with it. Nice to
know that musicians are the same the world over.

The only empty space in the entire train was the lavatory, to which I
eventually gained access. The main feature of it was a hole in the floor,
casually decorated with a piece of porcelain, and as I stood there more or less
successfully forecasting the jolts of the train I suddenly had a feeling that I
was being watched. That was ridiculous. I was the only person in there. I still
had a feeling I was under surveillance. It was then that my eyes fell on two
large sacks lying on the floor. From the neatly tied neck of each sack
projected the large head of a turkey; both were watching my operations with

beady and unblinking eyes. Who is this gringo? they seemed to be wondering. And what does he hope to find up this God-forsaken line to the back of beyond?

The answer, I suppose, is that I found the real Andes at last. This wasn't the highest anything in the world, and it didn't lead to Machu Picchu, and the Incas hadn't built the original railway stations, but this was the place in all Peru where I felt most at home, because it was least like home. I was deep in the middle of nowhere, surrounded by the most marvellous scenery imaginable, among people who were not even talking Spanish, most of them, but the native Quechua, and the best bit was that I wasn't going anywhere special. What seemed ages ago, but was only two days before, I had stood in Lima station staring up the line and wondering what amazing destination it led to. Now I knew.

Since my return I have sometimes been asked what I liked best about Peru and I have always said, the line from Huancayo to Huancavelica. Nobody has understood this. Nobody, that is, except that meteorologist from Lima airport. He too was on the train though we did not meet again until Huancavelica. He looked very happy.

'Isn't this marvellous?' he said.

We stood in the little dilapidated main square of the town, looking up at the black rim of the hills with the first stars coming out and the smell of some unidentified wayside snack tempting our nostrils, as the steam engine had done all day.

'Yes,' I said.

To the south, Peru is joined to Bolivia by Lake Titicaca, the highest navigable lake in the world. (Most of the navigating on the lake is done quite amiably and unspectacularly by the Indians in their reed boats. These take two days to build and lasted about six months. The glamorous side of navigation is provided by the SS *Ollanta*, a Hull-built steamer which crosses once a week. At night.) The port on the Peruvian side is Puno, a humdrum town, with a small museum. Its most eye-catching exhibition – to me, at least, who by then had had my fill of Inca Bits and Pieces – was a large photo on the stairs of the eight members of a 1937 expedition from Cambridge to survey the ecology of the lake. All keen and curious, they looked like scientific W H Audens, peering youthfully out at us in their khaki bush clothes. The effect on me was oddly nostalgic. The effect on Nick Lera, our chief cameraman and director, was electric.

'Good God!' he said, pointing at one of the faces. 'That's my science master! He *taught* me at school. And do you know what? For a special treat, he used to show us his film of Lake Titicaca which he'd shot when he was out here. How we used to groan when he got it out. And here I am, doing exactly the same thing . . .'

This little episode helps to sum up why, to some readers' surprise, I have virtually restricted myself to describing the Lima – Huancayo – Huancavelica journey. After that, I was to travel by train to Machu Picchu, to Cuzo and Puno, by the *Ollanta* to Guaqui in Bolivia and thence to La Paz. How could I remain silent on these places? Precisely because so many people have not remained silent; because it is such a well-travelled route that it needs no introduction from me. I was, to be honest, a little disappointed by Machu Picchu. The setting of this forgotten-and-found city of the Incas is indeed magnificent, perched on a breathtaking hill among mountains. Cuzco is a noble Spanish-type town with stirring Inca stonework still visible everywhere. And yet . . . and yet . . . I had read so much about Machu Picchu in advance that it never stirred me as it should have done. A feat of building, no doubt, but nothing compared to contemporary efforts such as Canterbury Cathedral.

Cuzco Cathedral is an impressive building, though somewhat gloomy in the Spanish vein. Here we spent an afternoon filming a huge picture of The Last Supper, notable chiefly for the food on the table, which is roast guinea pig (an Inca delicacy) and exotic fruits not mentioned in the Bible, such as bananas. One other curiosity of the painting is that eleven of the disciples are listening to Jesus, rapt; only Judas has turned away and is gazing out directly at the spectator. I might not have noticed this had not John Howarth, the assistant cameraman, turned to me in the dead still of the cathedral and whispered: 'Have you noticed there's always one bloody amateur who stares at the camera?'

To film in the cathedral we needed written permission from the Archbishop of Cuzco. To do anything, actually, we needed written permission, and Nick Lera had a sheaf of permits from the railways, the ministries, the tourist organisations, the police – anyone who might possibly otherwise object. These were never more necessary than one day when he was out in the country getting a lineside shot of the morning train from Cuzco. Unfortunately, between him and his vantage point there was a small police check-point, and he knew that if he was delayed there he would miss the train. Rashly he drove straight through. By the time the

A Vulcan Foundry Tender engine, built in the 1950s, chugs into La Paz

police had caught up with him, he had successfully filmed the train, and knew he could clear their suspicions by producing his permits. He put his hand in his pocket and found of course that this was the one day he had left them all behind. Ah, but not quite all. He had one letter of authorisation on him. It was from the Archbishop, allowing him to film The Last Supper. He handed it proudly to the police. They read it several times and, miraculously impressed, waved him on.

It is moments like this that come back to me when thinking of that last part of my journey, though none more so than our arrival in Bolivia which was fated to occur on the same day that the latest Bolivian revolution broke out. A military take-over, rather, as the generals had decided to annul the recent election of a left-wing president. All unsuspecting we disembarked from the SS *Ollanta*, bribed our way through customs and got on to the little railcar which was to take us across the high bleak altiplano and down to La Paz. Except that it was never to get there. In Viacha, a wayside town some twenty miles from La Paz, the train stopped and we were informed succinctly that it would continue as soon as the authorities deemed it safe which, as the Bolivians among us translated, meant never.

As by now a general strike has been called, a curfew announced and general chaos threatened, it was obvious that the ending we had planned for the film – a gentle perambulation round the English graveyard in La Paz, an elegiac visit to a graveyard of engines deep in the desert – would not now take place. While the other nationalities on the train reacted to the emergency in their own ways (the Germans methodically, the Dutch sensibly, the French by waving their arms, the Bolivians with re-signation), we sat and rued the lack of an ending. We could not even turn to the producer, who had gone separately by car to La Paz. Until it occurred to us that *this* was the ending. A revolution! Drama! What could be better? Obligingly, a lorry load of soldiers drove through the station waving their guns angrily at our cameras. Obligingly, another engine was derailed in front of ours, blocking our exit. Obligingly, the Bolivians stood around listening to their radios spouting out messages from the generals and playing military music non-stop.

For once, film and reality coincided; life was writing the script. And there at the trackside lay a bicycle. Bolivia . . . Butch Cassidy . . . put Kington on a bike and let him ride into the sunset, humming 'Raindrops Keep Falling . . .'

Thus it came to pass that the final shot of the film was my back riding into the distance, and thus it came to pass that everyone who has seen the film asks me what happened next. Quite simple. I encountered a convergence of two railway lines, had to stop and only then found out that the bicycle had no brakes. The bruises are still visible.

Later, when it was too dark to film, one of the Bolivian passengers came back with a lorry driver who promised for £40 or £50 to take us all down to La Paz. There was no haggling. All thirty of us jumped in(except for the French, who by a majority vote decided to stay in obedience to their Embassy's phoned instruction) and set off on one of the strangest journeys of my life. We were, literally, the only vehicle on the road, which seems not too odd on a country main road, but becomes eerie when you enter one of the biggest cities in South America. Near the town centre we began to encounter other vehicles. Tanks. Troop transport. The lorry driver lost his nerve and dumped us all at the first hotel we came to, which needless to say had no rooms vacant.

'The Bolivians are like children,' said the man in the lorry next to me, disgustedly. He should have known. He was a child psychiatrist from São Paulo in Brazil. He had come to Bolivia for a nice, quiet holiday away from the stress of city life. Now here he was in the middle of a revolution. The man on the other side of me was a black American, who had spent the last four years as the lead viola player in the São Paulo symphony orchestra. He was now on his way back to the States, to Philadelphia, to embark on a course of business studies, which he felt offered a more secure future than viola playing. They, of course, felt that anyone who had come from England to make a film on Bolivian railways was equally bizarre. The way I see it, actually, is that I know exactly where to make for the next time I take part in a TV film, part of a series I have provisionally entitled *Great Lorry Rides of the World.*

BRITAIN

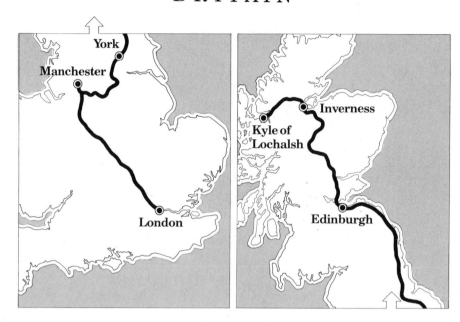

Confessions of a Train-Spotter

MICHAEL PALIN

THE TRAIN-SPOTTER

> 'Our father, which art in Heaven . . .
> Hallowed be thy name . . .'

Sunday 20 November 1955 . . .

> 'Thy Kingdom come . . .
> Thy will be done . . . On earth . . .'

A Bible class in Sheffield. Late afternoon.

> 'As it is in Heaven. Give us this
> day our daily bread . . .'

I want only one thing. I want to see the Thames–Clyde Express at the Midland Station and it's due in ten minutes. The station is a mile away and I've got no chance if Mr Turner slows up on the Lord's Prayer any more. I try to push the pace along by getting to the next line before anyone else. You can tell the train-spotters that way . . .

> 'And lead us not into . . . And lead
> us not into . . .'

The Thames–Clyde is an Anglo-Scottish express which, improbably, comes through Sheffield. The engine'll be a 'Jubilee' Class, and probably a familiar one from Leeds but you never know with an express which has already travelled nearly 300 miles that day.

> 'the power and the glory . . . for ever . . .'

Please hurry, *please*. I haven't copped a 'Jub' for a week and a half.

> 'and . . . ever . . .'

It's probably passing through Tinsley now . . . with eleven packed coaches and the smoke shooting high above the factories . . .

> . . . Amen . . .
> . . . Amen . . .

Move fast. Hand in my books . . . deftly avoid all contact with fellow human beings re stacking chairs or prayer meetings or who should give out the hymn books next week. Polite smiles and goodbyes, ease towards the door and *voom*! . . tie and coat tails flapping, shoes (worn down at the edges by too much of this sort of thing) skidding and sliding across wet roads and pavements . . . through Paradise Square, up Angel Street, across Fargate, narrowly missing death from an oncoming bus, cut through Change Alley, swerve down towards Pond Street, past the bus depot and Midland Station is in sight. Neat, restrained, low stone façade. Still no tell-tale plumes of smoke or hiss of recently discharged steam to indicate the arrival of an express, so I redouble my efforts – flat feet thudding over cobbles, sprinting the last 200 yards with such vigour that I can't be many seconds outside the world record. I finally tumble into the station, fumble for a penny, grab a platform ticket and thunder along the resounding wood-floored bridge to platform 8. I can taste blood in my throat, and I'm gasping for breath like a freshly-landed fish but I'm dead on time. A loudspeaker above my head crackles . . . 'The Thames–Clyde Express from Glasgow St Enoch is

running approximately fifty-eight minutes late . . . fifty-*eight* minutes
late . . .'

Come to think of it, it always *was* late on a Sunday, but that never
stopped me from risking life and limb to be there just in case. And anyway,
waiting was all part of the excitement; the pleasure of anticipating the
arrival of an express which had been in Glasgow at breakfast time, crossed
the desolate Pennine moors at lunchtime and was now somewhere in
Yorkshire heading towards this platform as autumn dusk fell.

Meanwhile there were always other things to see. Odd engines clanking
to and fro rather haphazardly. Apart from shunters (mostly tank engines)
there were locals pulled by 3MTs and 4MTs. If there was one I hadn't seen
before it was underlined in my Ian Allan book. This was known as a 'cop'.
But these were not particularly glamorous engines nor were the 5.31 to
Barnsley or the colliery empties from Rotherham particularly glamorous
trains to pull, and I was, despite my appearance in those days, quite
susceptible to a bit of glamour, so a train with a title on its headboard, and
name and destination emblazoned on the sides of its coaches, was worth
waiting at least fifty-eight minutes for.

Fifty-eight minutes later I have 'copped' 40557 and 73069 and I'm dying to
go to the lavatory. There has been no further announcement about the
Thames–Clyde Express. I fidget a lot and walk round in ever-widening
circles and re-read for the twentieth time the advert for this year's Lyceum
Panto, starring Albert Modley and Ken Platt, until I can't bear it any
longer. I race to the nearest 'gents', but no sooner am I at the enamel than I
hear: 'The train now approaching platform 8 is the Thames–Clyde Express
. . .' A brief nervous spasm grips me . . . a frightful sweat of indecision . . .
but my body is stronger than my mind and I just stand there praying that
there might be a last-minute signal failure or a sheep on the line or a rail
strike. Veins are standing out on my temples as I fight my lone battle to
accelerate nature. I hear for the first time the approaching clank and
rumble, the bustling of an important express. How I wish I hadn't bought
that second cup of Bovril. Now there is a reverberating tone to the clank
and rumble . . . a perceptible shudder passes through the stone floor,
indicating that the express has entered the bounds of the station. Now only
six fly buttons separate me from the train I love. The top two are sacrificed
and I race out into the throng of anxious, irritable passengers just as the
steaming, sweating bulk of the engine darkens the platform and sweeps
magnificently by . . . followed (and here in my amazement and delight I

Train-spotters race beside a steam engine as it draws to a halt

run into an unexpectedly resilient old lady) by yet *another* steaming beast. A double-header! Rare on this stretch of the line and probably a result of one of the two breaking down. The passengers I push my joyful way through bear expressions ranging from weary patience, through anger to downright despair. They're cold, they're late, and every last space on the train looks to have been taken by cold and late passengers from Leeds. But up at the end of the platform, beneath the signals, where only those who love trains (or work on them) ever go, there is none of the bitter hopelessness that grips the traveller, there is just the quiet delight of a twelve-year-old train-spotter, confronted on this cold and inhospitable November Sunday by not one, but two, named engines that he's never seen before . . . 45717 *Dauntless* and 45670 *Howard of Effingham.* And there's still the 6.25 from London to look forward to. And that's only eighteen minutes late.

Between the ages of twelve and fourteen I persevered very thoroughly with the spotter's craft. I graduated from the unsensational homeliness of Sheffield Midland, with its friendly Jubilees and Black Fives (which to this day form my archetypal image of the steam locomotive) to the East Coast main line at Retford, which was about a four and tenpenny return from Sheffield. Here there was an embarrassment of riches . . . a dozen named expresses a day, flying through at speeds which made the Thames–Clyde look like a bookend. It was tremendous entertainment. The locomotives were bigger and sleeker than anything at Sheffield. There were the Gresley A4s streamlined like bullets, solid A3s like the *Flying Scotsman*, the majestic A2s with windshields, and three or four times a day there were Pullman trains. On Pullmans we used to spot the names of the coaches. I'm proud to say I have them all apart from *Thelma* and *Ursula*. Even in 1956 these coaches looked hopelessly, wonderfully out of date. When I'd finished my soggy pork pie and was wiping the ink and fluff off a half-sucked Fox's Glacier mint that I'd found in the long-forgotten recesses of a trouser pocket, I used to envy those composed and urbane diners sitting in *Agatha*, being pulled by *Meg Merrilies* on an express called Queen of the Scots. (The nearest equivalent these days is to sit in an Inter-City restaurant car behind Class 254 (DMB) power car No. 254018 on the 17.15.)

In those days British Railways regions were still distinguished from each other very clearly. Colours and engine design differed sharply in various parts of the country. In 1956 I went by train to a summer camp near Swanage and I shall never forget the fascination of entering the malachite green world of the Southern Region, and finding a train that had left Sheffield behind the obligatory Jubilee was being hauled out of Blandford Forum by a quite unfamiliar, chunkily streamlined green beast of the unfortunately named wc class. At Bournemouth I couldn't wait to scuttle up the platform and, approaching somewhat warily, take a closer look at this wholly foreign animal. It was called, rather demurely, *Bude*. The number was 34006. So underlinings began to appear on the previously virgin sr pages of my Ian Allan Combined Volume (1955) . . . To a mind conditioned by Greek warriors, English naval battles, racehorses and Walter Scott heroes was now added the wonderful world of N.15 Class 4–6–0s – *Sir Gareth* – *Sir Urre of the Mount* (try saying that after a few Diet Pils), *Sir Harry Le Fiske Lake*. I even saw 30782 *Sir Brian* (a prophetic 'cop' for one who has since been involved in *Monty Python and the Holy Grail* and *The Life of Brian*).

Certainly no one can accuse the Southern Region of taking the easy way out when they decided to name the N.15s after Arthurian heroes. Was anyone aware that there were forty-four engines in the class? Do *you* know forty-four Arthurian heroes? Imagine the scene (as they say in comedy shows)

One class of engines was called after private schools

amidst the din of welding, riveting and drilling, the dust and dirt and noise, the swirling fumes and flying sparks, of Eastleigh locomotive works, a harassed foreman with hot metal dangling past his left ear and a freshly completed class N.15 at his elbow is straining at the telephone with pencil stub and a piece of thumb-blackened paper.

'30811's ready . . .' he says. 'What's the name?'

A man in the Bodleian Library, his gloved finger in the first edition of *Morte d'Arthur*, replies, '. . . Sir Meliot . . .'

'What mate?'

'Mel*iot* . . .'

'Bellyhot . . . ?'

'No . . . no no . . . *Mel*iot.'

'Sorry mate you'll have to speak up, they're making engines in here . . .'

'Sir Meliot . . . That's M . . . E . . . L . . . I . . . O . . . T.'

'All right, got it . . . Sir Meliot . . . thanks mate.'

'Wait! Wait! There's more. Sir Meliot de Logres.'

'de what?'

'. . . de Logres . . . that's L . . . O . . . G . . .'

'Oh, hell, can't we just call it Brian?'

But there was a *Sir Meliot de Logres*, I know. I copped it.

In what other country in the world would you find an entire class of engines named after private schools? Class V. 4–4–0 was called *Shrewsbury* and it is ironic that it was my years spent at Shrewsbury School, between 1957 and 1961, which nearly cured me of railways altogether. At first it seemed too good to be true – a school on both the Western and London Midland region. To an underprivileged Sheffield spotter it was like unlocking Fort Knox. I went mad on new notebooks, new pencils, the most up-to-date loco-books. I polished my Ian Allan LMS badge and my ER badge and sent away for a WR badge. But that was as far as it went. As soon as I started scribbling at Crewe, I was aware of a few raised eyebrows and quickly hidden smiles, and it didn't take me very long to realise that in the exalted company of public schoolboys my behaviour was distinctly uncool. Never one to be swayed by pressure of convention or the vagaries of fashion I gave up train-spotting almost immediately. Shrewsbury Station remained a largely unvisited Mecca, Crewe became a bore and to this day I only have seven Western Region numbers underlined in my book.

For many years after that railways became a dull necessity mainly associated with separations . . . tearful departures and tearful arrivals. I found myself waiting impatiently for the ever-late Thames–Clyde Express, so my elder sister could be seen off to her work in London and I could get away from the station and back home to the Goon Show repeats. I hardly noticed the phasing out of steam in the early 1960s, and when I was forced to spend any of my precious student grant on rail travel it was generally to throw myself on the last train from Paddington to Oxford, after extracting the final ounces of enjoyment from a weekend of London delights. I didn't care what was on the front of the train, so long as it got me to Oxford. Which it did, but only just. The 12.05 from Paddington was a slow, cold, miserable train, only run, I think, to take condemned stock up to some knacker's yard near Worcester. There was little or no light and little or no speed. The train slunk out of Paddington glumly, like a stray cat being turned out of a warm house, and continued in a surly way to Slough and Reading and Didcot, where it stopped and started in a series of in-explicably violent jerks, traumatically waking anyone who had had the rare good fortune to get to sleep. It was said that a Professor of History at my college had died on this train, and I'm not surprised, there were times in the eerie half-light when the yellowed and bleary faces of travellers made Doré's engravings look like keep-fit adverts. I was always mildly surprised that it reached Oxford at all, but even more surprised that there were some hopeful souls still left aboard who actually expected it to reach Worcester. One thing was for sure – the very last thing in my mind was the number of the engine quietly steaming at the front.

All I yearned for at that time was my own car so that I could avoid railway travel altogether. Between 1962 and 1968, as the momentous years of the

Beeching plan, rail closures and the creeping extinction of steam went by, I only travelled by train as a last resort.

Then quite suddenly my interest in railways revived. In the same month as we formed the Monty Python team (May 1969) my wife gave me Cecil J. Allen's *Titled Trains of Great Britain* as a birthday present. I glanced through the book in a cursory fashion, then again more slowly and finally very slowly indeed, drinking greedily of such information as I could find about the departure times of The Fenman or the saga of name changes on The Cornish Riviera Express. I pored over photos of the Master Cutler leaving Marylebone or the Royal Scot at speed, and all the old responses were awakened.

There were various symptoms of this renewed awareness. I took my son at some suitable age, like seventeen and a half months, to walk up and down St Pancras Station on a sunny autumn Sunday. Not to catch the train, just to catch the atmosphere. I gingerly bought another railway book consisting entirely of pictures of the age of steam, and I wallowed in it quite shamelessly when no one was looking. I began to use the railways again in preference to the car. I had to make regular visits to Southwold to visit my parents, and I found that I became much more tolerant and tolerable to all concerned if I went by train rather than fighting my way out of London on the roads. The journey on the 9.30 from Liverpool Street to Ipswich is now a nine or ten times yearly ritual. I eat one of the most civilised breakfasts to be had outside of one's own home, I work at a script and I still have enough time left on the return journey to read half a novel. When we filmed up in Scotland I would always volunteer to take the night sleeper rather than the early morning plane. (The sleeper to Fort William provides the quite wondrous delight of going to sleep somewhere near Tring and waking up near Tyndrum, in the middle of a vast empty wildness of mountains and lochs. Never do I clean my teeth more thoroughly than in that initial ten-minute trance as I stare out of my sleeper window and find Scotland all over the place.)

But there were still significant differences between Palin the responsible mid-thirty-year-old with three children and a mortgage who happened to quite like trains and Palin the pimply spotter. Palin Now still didn't make the once-obligatory trip up the platform to look at the engine, Palin Now didn't possess an up-to-date Ian Allan ABC of British Locomotives. Palin Now didn't really know the difference between modern engine classes.

Palin Now could not recite from intimate knowledge of names and numbers. Then came the phone call.

It was at the very end of November 1979. I was at my desk wrestling with the comedic possibilities of two ducks, a bishop and a sailor with three wooden legs when the phone rang for the twelfth time in an hour. It was a man with a northern accent, which stalled my irritation at once. He was a producer for BBC Manchester, who had heard me defending railways on a Radio 1 phone-in the night before and was wondering if I were interested, by any remote chance, in writing and presenting a documentary for BBC 2 about a railway journey through Britain. With commitments to write two films, a book, a book review, an interview with the *Sunday Times* and present the *Melody Maker* Pop Awards – all by five o'clock – I was only momentarily interested; it was like being offered a nice sit down when you're on the eighteenth mile of a marathon. But I couldn't bring myself to say no outright, so I promised to ring back in a couple of days, put the phone down with routine briskness and thought nothing else of the offer for at least three seconds. Then a remarkable thing happened. A metaphorical shaft of clear golden light shone suddenly and with piercing clarity through the metaphorical gloom of the train-spotter turned comedy-writer's addled brain. Reason and good sense dispersed before the intensity of this light, furrows on the brow expanded and vanished, tight lips relaxed into a smile, chair tipped back and shoulders widened. It took me less than twenty-five seconds to realise that I had just been offered Something I Really Wanted To Do. In less than sixty seconds I dialled BBC Manchester and took the job.

Anyone with any knowledge of railway history will appreciate the fact that the BBC Producer who rang me was called Stephenson (well actually that was the way it was pronounced, in fact he spells it Stephinson). Not only was his name Stephinson but he actually lived, slept, ate and washed up within inches of the Manchester–Newcastle main line. And not only did he live within inches of a main line, he also sounded a very pleasant fellow and I detected from his tone that we would have a rather good time. Add all this to the offer of a Great Railway Journey and I was hooked. So hooked that I abandoned work on the Python film script for that day and dug around in the recesses of my work-room for books, maps, routes, timetables, pictures and anything by O S Nock. I cleared out a mound of unsold *Ripping Yarns* books and started a railway shelf. Friends were a little mystified that I was proposing to spend over two months of my year on a railway documentary, and my financial manager was downright horrified. I enjoyed both reactions greatly and set to buying pictures of trains and back copies of the *Railway Magazine* for research.

I discovered that the literature of railways is extensive and meticulous – the humblest branch line has its own bibliography, often in several volumes. There are authoritative works on signalling, points and bogie design. If you were to write a *History of Brass Screws in the Third Class Coaches of the Cirencester and Swindon Joint Railway between 1904 and 1905* you could probably retire on the proceeds. Mind you, if you had some of the brass screws themselves you'd be even better off for railway fittings are also big business. Behind Euston station is a loft full of such railway bric-à-brac. It's called Collectors Corner and you can buy porters' caps and guards' lamps and tickets and buttons and track layouts and oddly shaped steel lumps whose purpose is debatable but whose origin was Birmingham Snow Hill station. Head boards, shed codes, bent 'Gentlemen' signs (the *signs* are bent, not the gentlemen) in GWR chocolate and cream. Whenever I have been to Collectors Corner there was always a fair-sized crowd sifting through these railway relics. It's clear that an awful lot of British Rail is passing quite steadily into private hands. I have the feeling that a complete sub-network of steam railways is being gradually built up complete with its own lines, locomotives, signal boxes, signals, uniforms, and manual level-crossing gates, just waiting for the day when passengers finally rebel against the latest fare rise and steam returns triumphant.

As each day of research on my Great Railway Journey went by I found myself dipping further into childhood memories and when I found myself at Euston Station on the first day of shooting it seemed entirely natural that I should buy the most up-to-date Ian Allan ABC (now no longer called the ABC of British Railways Locomotives, but, rather drily, *British Rail Motive Power*), and it seemed entirely natural that I should amble up to look at the engine before the journey began, and seeing that it was a Class 86/2, No. 86218 'Planet', it seemed entirely natural that I should note this with a pencil mark in my ABC. Almost without noticing it, I had become a train-spotter again.

THE JOURNEY

The Journey, not the arrival matters;
the voyage, not the landing

Paul Theroux *The Old Patagonian Express*

The route I was to take and the trains I was to take it on had already been chosen for me. I was to head north from Euston, visit the Rainhill Trials, take a special excursion from Manchester to York, hauled by *Flying Scotsman*, tootle around the museum at York, take a detour over the North York Moors Railway and the Esk Valley Line, visit such seminal spots in railway history as Darlington and Newcastle, look at the Newcastle Metro, and take the HST to Edinburgh (in the cab if possible). From Edinburgh, across the Highlands to Inverness and Kyle of Lochalsh, then by ferry to Mallaig and Mallaig to Fort William and Fort William to Glasgow and finally by APT to London Euston. Though neglecting the Southern and Western Regions it was a pretty bold attempt to cover the country by rail – and for a while I was simply intoxicated with the opportunities it presented. I was to ride on nine different trains (diesel, electric and steam) and a ferry. I was to travel 1400 miles, twice on the footplate, on the fastest train, over the highest summit, through the most beautiful scenery, behind the most famous steam engine – and as far afield as the Isle of Skye.

Anxious to be realistic I packed a suitcase containing several changes of costume which weighed a ton and nearly drove me to distraction. By the time we reached Scotland I honestly contemplated a sequence in which the traveller, bitten in the guard's van by a rabid Shetland pony, would hurl his suitcase out of the window in the pass of Killiecrankie during a severe bout of manic hysteria.

But all that was later. As we left Euston, I was still deeply in love with the whole experience. Not that Euston is the slightest bit inspiring. It is the functional, practical, cost-effective station of the mid-twentieth century. It does not try to enlist the emotions in the same way as St Pancras, half a mile down the road. Euston exists with the sole purpose of getting as many bodies in and out of it as quickly as possible. Of course the railways have to change and adapt, but as we slid away from the bare concrete platforms beneath grey steel gantries and over litter-strewn sleepers I thought again of the words in the prospectus for this same railway, published in 1838.

The steam Engine and the Railway are not merely facilitating the transport of merchandise; they are not merely shortening the duration of journeys; or administering to the supply of wants; they are creating new demands for knowledge; they are fertilising the intellectual as well as the material waste; they are removing the impediments which obscurity, or remoteness, or poverty may have heretofore opposed to the emerging of real merit. They are supplying you in the mere facility of locomotion, with a new motive for classical study.

It sounds a bit overblown but the Victorians had a great pride in public works. Technology was something new and admirable and noble. Now the tendency is to accept much lower standards of design in public buildings for the sake, we are told, of cost.

But the modernisation of the trains themselves is a different matter. Only a masochist (or railway fan) would really prefer the belching smoke, flying black smuts and rattling ride of the old steam trains to the smooth swiftness of the electrics which almost unnoticeably accelerate to 100 miles an hour before we've even passed Wembley Stadium.

We're rocketing through north-west London's trim 1930s suburbia when I hear the first crackle of an impending announcement. 'This is your guard speaking' . . . (longish pause) . . . 'I'm not the proper guard. He didn't turn up' . . . (slightly shorter pause, but increasing bitterness of tone) . . . 'I just happened to be walking along the platform at the time . . . that's all' . . . (very long pause). Then, contemptuously, 'This is the 9.55 to Manchester-callingatStokeMacclesfieldand . . . Stockport.' Click. If you've ever been subjected to the bland pre-recorded instructions that airline travel is plagued with, or if you are just interested in the rich variety of human experience, then you cannot but be heartily grateful for whatever bureaucratic oversight it was to allow guards to make up their own announcements. To hear all the stations to Inverness announced in an enthusiastic Bengali accent is to relive the golden age of the Raj, and I once travelled down from Newcastle with a West Indian guard, who announced to us . . . 'This train will be four minutes early arriving at Stevenage . . . four minutes early at Stevenage . . . (pause) . . . Let's keep it that way!' This earned a spontaneous round of applause. Less satisfactorily, I have heard, 'This train is running late owing to the train in front,' or the even more unnerving, 'Ladies and Gentlemen, we are just approaching – no, sorry'.

We are out of London now and running alongside the Grand Union canal, which only existed for thirty-three years before the railway came to nip its short-lived boom in the bud. The train is fairly empty. The director is anxious to film me amongst typical British passengers. It would have to be today that the four people in the seat behind me are all Rabbis. As we flash past Berkhamsted, birthplace of G. Greene, I pay silent mental homage.

Then a lady brings along the coffee service. This is in two stages. First a small plastic container with a thin sprinkling of brown powder in the bottom, and just when in desperation you are about to swallow this neat, hot water arrives.

Although the first trains began running in 1830, it wasn't until 1879 that the Great Northern Railway Company first introduced a dining-car service. Before that you had to rely on swift work at the occasional buffet stops. In 1862 The Railway Travellers Handy Book provided a whole section on the art of eating a four-course meal in twenty minutes. For instance, when ordering soup it advised you to shout 'Soup!' rather than the polite but time-consuming 'a basin of soup please'. Maybe Charles Dickens had a bad experience at one of these buffets for he described a typical railway fare of his time as 'glutinous lumps of gristle and grease, sponge cakes that turn to sand in the mouth' and 'brown patties composed of unknown animals within'.

Looking outside again I see we're passing the spot where one of British Rail's many world records was set. The record for lifting large sums of money out of trains. At Bridego Bridge in Buckinghamshire a Euston mail train was stopped by a false signal and relieved of £2¼ million. It will always be *the* Great Train Robbery.

As the lulling pattern of embankment, cutting, tunnel, embankment, cutting, tunnel, embankment is about to send me quietly to sleep I'm aware of how much we take the engineering of such lines for granted. The laying of this one was under the supervision of George Stephenson's son Robert and in the mid 1830s they certainly didn't take his achievement for granted. As one contemporary wrote of the London Birmingham Railway: 'If we estimate its importance by the labour alone which has been expended upon it, perhaps the great Chinese wall might compete with it, but when we consider the great outlay of capital which it has required, together with the unprecedented engineering difficulties, the gigantic work of the Chinese sinks wholly into the shade.'

Once the line has parted company with the Grand Union Canal there really isn't much to catch the eye out of either window until Manchester Piccadilly is reached. Manchester Piccadilly doesn't catch the eye either, being one of the awful 'new' stations of the post-steam era, but midway between here and Liverpool, at Rainhill, I stopped off at the remarkable recreation of the Rainhill Trials of 1829 when Stephenson's *Rocket* beat all opposition (including one locomotive powered by a horse on a treadmill)

The *Flying Scotsman*

and created such an impression that railways were finally taken seriously. A year later in 1830, the world's first regular passenger service, from Liverpool to Manchester, began. It's interesting to note the careful 'ecological' provisions written into the rules of the Trials. Not only were the engines not allowed to exceed 10 mph but they had also to 'effectively consume their own smoke'.

If Rainhill was my first glimpse of mass adoration of railways (for there were upwards of 30,000 people to watch the celebrations in June 1980), then our journey to York behind *Flying Scotsman* was my first really close look at today's enthusiasts. True railway buffs love *all* engines – short, fat, squat, long – rumbling smelly diesels or swiftly silent electrics, but most of all they love steam, and the most famous steam engine of them all is *Flying Scotsman*. It was built in 1923 for the newly formed LNER – London and North Eastern Railway. It was retired in 1963, but it is still going strong thanks to a variety of believers who've put their money into it, from Alan Pegler to its present owner Bill MacAlpine. *Flying Scotsman* at full steam against a backdrop of woods and green fields provides one of the most enduring images of England, the sort that made the Englishman abroad go misty-eyed in the evenings and reach sadly for the whisky bottle. It's the England of *Thomas The Tank Engine* and *The Railway Children*, when the trains were always friendly. Today the *Flying Scotsman*, one of 500 preserved steam locos in Britain, is taking me from Manchester to York and it's a special excursion for the faithful.

'Sight, sound and emotion' are the three main elements in the appreciation of the steam railway locomotive according to fellow passenger George Hinchcliffe, a warm, friendly, humorous and helpful man who runs SLOA – the Steam Locomotive Operators Association. To prove his point every window of this train was occupied throughout the journey by worshippers in goggles holding the most sophisticated sound-gathering protrusions to catch every nuance of the *Scotsman's* performance. At every station and atop every bridge and along every embankment between Manchester and Sheffield the fans were ranged like Sioux warriors in a western, armed with Nikons instead of tomahawks. I was amazed by the size of following this sturdy, unflashy steam engine has acquired, and by the intensity of the railfans' devotion. I was also a little chastened. I realised that I was merely a dabbler. To those who notice every milepost, every gradient, every click of the wheels . . . who calculate running times every minute of the journey, who are constantly writing, noting, comparing and analysing, I am a mere dilettante, a fair-weather follower, who, when the chips are down, would rather listen to the Beatles than B-17s.

But my moment of personal homage to steam was still to come. At York I turned off from the main line to see how one of the country's sixty-seven private railway lines was faring. The North Yorkshire Moors Railway runs eighteen miles of track between Pickering and Grosmont – a line which was closed by British Rail in 1975 on the advice of Dr Beeching and re-opened by the Duchess of Kent four years later. It's a most beautiful stretch of line and on it came almost the supreme moment of my entire journey, when I was asked to ride in the cab of a Stanier Black Five. The Black Fives were the workhorses at Sheffield Midland during my spotting days, and though there are many more glamorous engines there was something straight and direct and unpretentious about them. I felt at home with them and can remember fiercely defending their honour against taunts from better-travelled spotters. So to see a Black Five gently steaming at Pickering Station in 1980 was like encountering an old friend, and the good

The North Yorkshireman on the North York Moors Railway at Grosmont

people from the North York Moors Railway, who look after the engine, let me ride on the footplate for the last trip of the day. Most of the cloud had disappeared leaving an evening of piercing sunshine, and right from the thundering start it was clear that the driver and fireman were out to impress. The driver leapt up and down on the regulator like Nijinsky and the fireman heaved and hurled the coal in a strong consistent rhythm until we'd built up a head of steam which took us along well beyond the permitted 35 mph. The driver's eyes twinkled with mischievous delight and there was a tangible feeling of exhilaration on the footplate as we tore up the gradient towards Goathland. It was a satisfaction that can never be experienced in the clinical cabs of diesel or electrics – the satisfaction of seeing a supreme effort of human skill and strength combined to realise the full potential of a machine.

After that I was almost blasé about riding in the cab of a High Speed Train between Newcastle and Edinburgh. Though we were racing at 115 mph I noticed the lack of one of George Hinchcliffe's three elements of loco appreciation – sound. And I missed it. At one point a pheasant ran slap bang into the front of the train, which led one of the drivers (there have to be two) to tell the story of a friend of his on a Northumbrian branch line, who at one particular stretch on the outward journey would flush corn down the toilets, and on the return take his pick of however many pheasants had been unable to get out of the way in time. The High Speed Trains reach Edinburgh from London in four and a half hours. They're reasonably comfortable, but the seats are harder and the windows higher than on the Mark II coaches.

The Inter-City 125 service sells itself on speed and frequency. In the 1930s the LNER, which ran the London to Edinburgh service, tried to sell its services in much more elaborate fashion. On various trains and for various periods they tried hairdressing facilities, a cinema coach, radio headphones, showers, Louis XIV armchairs in the dining room, a travelling library, a ladies retiring coach, itinerant newspaper and magazine sellers, observation cars, and a cocktail bar with a range of twenty cocktails, including a Flying Scotsman for a shilling. It's interesting that the 1930s – a decade which one tends to associate with economic depression and international instability – produced the last great attempts at conspicuous luxury and extravagant show in the transport world. It was the decade of busy transatlantic liners and lushly equipped airships, and on the railways of streamlined, specially painted expresses like Silver Link and Coronation Scot. LNER and LMS were fighting for speed as well as luxury, and the streamlining of engines was an attempt to push steam power to its limits. In the years just before the Second World War records were set for steam which were never again repeated. *Mallard* (now in York Railway Museum) reached a world record of 126 mph in July 1938, and in 1937 an LNER express called Coronation ran from London to York at an average of nearly seventy-two miles an hour and to Edinburgh in only six hours.

There really was no great breakthrough in train speeds until 1977 when the High Speed Trains were introduced on the east-coast mainline. Once again streamlining helped, but the strength of two diesel-power cars surpassed anything a shovelling fireman could achieve, and soon the Inter-City 125 service was hitting an average of ninety-one miles an hour to York and reaching Edinburgh in almost four and a half hours. The difference nowadays is that there are no cinema cars or hairdressing saloons or travelling libraries, or special liveries. More sadly, there are no headboards, announcing that the train is The Coronation or The Silver Link or even The Scarborough Flyer or The Heart of Midlothian. All of which I'm not ashamed to say I miss. Mind you, I have recently noticed encouraging signs of revisionism in this matter. The names The Aberdonian and The Flying Scotsman and The Talisman still occur in the official 1980/81 Passenger Timetable, and on stickers placed discreetly on some windows of selected HST doors. Whether or not they have been placed there by British Rail hands I'm not sure, but I have the feeling it could be the thin end of quite an imaginative wedge.

We glide across Robert Stephenson's Royal Border Bridge and through Berwick-on-Tweed – a town with a schizophrenic relationship with both England and Scotland, and a history of administrative independence which has resulted in Berwick being technically still at war with Russia. The scenery of Scotland takes over now, and causes me to 'ooh!' and 'ah!' like a goldfish for the next 600 miles. From Berwick up to Dunbar the line plays around the top of the cliffs, with a sweeping view out over the grey North Sea, and occasionally sight of an almost sheer drop down the cliffs to a wave-pounded beach or a tiny fishing village. This latter view is highly recommended on High Speed Trains as a spinal exercise as the windows are set just a little too high for the coventionally slumped sightseer.

The railway approach in to Edinburgh, like the centre of Edinburgh itself, is very grand. There is something gravely welcoming in the way in which the train slips into Waverley Station, beneath the stern eye of the Castle and the big, respectable buildings which flank the sides of the hill. It's rather like a Victorian grandmother lifting her skirts to provide warm shelter for a tired child. And the station must be unique in Britain in that it took its title from a novel, Sir Walter Scott's *Waverley*.

Edinburgh does live up to the most romantic ideals of a 'destination'. Indeed it seems an anti-climax to contemplate leaving it for anywhere else. So I stayed overnight in the massive black rock of the North British Hotel, one of the two imposing railway hotels that mark either end of Princes

A north-bound train crosses the River Tweed at Berwick-on-Tweed

Street. It was built by the North British Railway in 1903 to outdo in size, scale and splendour anything the Caledonian Railway could put up. Its style of decoration is modestly described in an early brochure as 'a free rendering of the Renaissance period'. It stands ten storeys high – six of them above and four of them below Princes Street. A lift carries me up from platform level to the hotel and I step out into an arrival hall which again I think can only be adequately described by reference to the 1903 brochure. 'A large and handsome room, of noteworthy aspect and design, divided into six compartments by reeded alabaster columns supported by pedestals or set on dados of Numidian marble, with brèche-clair bases and corniches . . . while the floor is of slabs of Sicilian marble.' And this is quite restrained compared to other parts of the building such as the Palm Court, (or Lounge) crowned with an octagonal dome filled with stained glass, supported on massive pillars with wonderful sprouting plasterwork capitals and Titanic-style mirrors.

In the morning I purposely avoid the lift in order to walk to my breakfast down the grand staircase past armorial bearings in stained glass and down stairs wide enough for three simultaneous Busby Berkeley dance routines. How long will the evidence of such exuberant extravagance survive? It belongs to the Golden Railway Age, when the car was still an awkward fledgling and trains seemed to have transport sewn up. Now we have High Speed Trains I can't help feeling it's a short step to High Speed Hotels. I suppose it depends on what you look for in a hotel. If it's an instant bed and instant coffee and a telex machine it doesn't really matter to you how freely the Renaissance period is rendered, but if you want a superbly comfortable bed with linen sheets and a down pillow, carefully cooked and carefully chosen food and drink, baths the size of small swimming pools, and old-fashioned personal service, then railway hotels are the ones to choose.

I left Edinburgh on the 9.45 to Inverness, with the prospect of a ride across the Highlands between breakfast and lunch, and, all being well, to the shores of the Isle of Skye for supper. The day ahead promised some beguiling 'firsts' – my first ride over the Highland Line across the highest summit on the British Rail network (Druimuachdar at 1484 feet), my first time as far north as Inverness (575 miles from London), my first visit to a Highland Games and first chance to experience the delights of the Lochalsh Hotel, which advises in its blurb that after your meal you should 'stroll into the bar where lined up on the counter will be one of the most impressive selections of whiskies you've ever seen' (eighty to be precise – sixty of them pure malts). So my anticipation is keen as our train, bearing a back-pack carrying army of hikers slides away from Waverley Station, beneath the elegant classical façade of the Scottish National Gallery, surely the noblest building ever to adorn the top of a railway tunnel, and curling round close to the base of the hefty rock, with the castle looming a hundred feet above us, we gradually pull away from Edinburgh.

Within a dozen miles an impending sense of anti-climax at leaving such a city is dispelled as we reach the wide sweep of the Firth of Forth and on to one of the greatest monuments of the railway in Britain or anywhere else – the Forth Bridge. It has two spans, each 1710 feet long, and is an intricate and powerful piece of construction which quite thoroughly upstages its sixty-years younger brother upstream – the spare and elegant Forth Road Bridge. Infuriatingly the real beauty of the bridge cannot really be seen from the train, and it wasn't until I saw the shots taken from our helicopter that my breath was finally taken away. But there is a great excitement to be felt in the train as you rumble out over a 250-foot sheer drop to the sea below, with the girders and columns of the bridge flashing by in fantastical patterns. It was built ninety years ago, and must have seemed even more stupendous in an age when the pony and trap was still the most common form of transport. Its designers and builders were Sir John Fowler and Sir Benjamin Baker, whose names should be on any railway roll of honour alongside an engineer from Inverness called Joseph Mitchell. Mitchell it was who designed and built 104 miles of the Highland Railway between Perth and Inverness in less than two years for £8860 per mile; nowadays it would cost a million a mile at least. Even allowing for the fact that Mitchell must have used a mighty army of navvies, it's another colossal achievement of design and construction.

Unfortunately there are less colossal achievements from our Class 47 locos today, and after Perth the journey becomes a bit of a ramble. At Blair Atholl we are stopped for an unconscionable time and, as tends to happen with stopped trains, the place soon becomes a hotbed of rumour. There's only hot water in the two rear coaches, or there's a herd of reindeer on the line or one engine's broken down and the nearest replacement is in Middlesborough.

By the time I've read every advert on Blair Atholl Station twelve times I'm beginning to think it's going to take us longer to travel the line than it took Joseph Mitchell to build it. At last we move, not terribly rapidly, but then we are beginning a long ascent to the pass of Drumochter. The countryside around is bleak rather than grand and I look in vain for typical Highland scenery – mountains soaring above me, sunlit lochs and pine forests, that sort of thing. To make matters worse the A9 main road runs alongside and we're being overtaken by a Morris Traveller with a bed on top. I was told on good authority by a railway contact that all BR drivers are unofficially encouraged to go flat out when there's a main road running alongside, to show the opposition a clean pair of heels, boost morale, that sort of thing. But today on Drumochter Pass we're being passed by everything, and eventually we run into Inverness nearly an hour late.

Inverness Station is a let-down too. Or maybe I've just been idealising this part of the journey too much. Or perhaps I've been sold too much of the tourist image of the Highlands as clean, fresh and impressive. Inverness Station was certainly none of these when I was there. A plucky attempt to provide flower tubs seemed to have misfired as most of the Travelling Public clearly thought that the tubs were litter bins and that the flowers and earth inside had been thrown away by somebody. The platforms were just parking places for goods barrows and the forecourt was full of disconsolate back-packers and the occasional drunk lurching dangerously

Crossing beneath the girders of the Forth
Rail Bridge which was built 90 years ago

around, obviously wrestling with the knotty problem of whether or not he could afford 3p to throw up in the toilet.

I walked out into the town. It was a busy Saturday afternoon and the only shops that were empty were kilt sellers. I ventured in and looked through an enormously long list designed to reassure almost anyone that there *was* a clan tartan for them. I learnt that the Cohens were in fact an offshoot of the Robertsons, the Schmidts of the MacFadyeans and Ibn Ali Ben Sauds were very distant Campbells. But of Palin no sign. I was advised to try the shop down the road, but I felt bitterly let down and went to a Highland Games instead.

Here the Highlands really began to brighten up. Everyone was terribly nice or terribly pissed, and very often both. There were little kids doing the sword dance with great skill, there were pipers trying to outpipe each other and running races and cycling races and in the middle of all this there were men throwing hammers and heaving twenty-pound weights and tossing cabers. I asked someone if there was much of a casualty rate at games like these. Were pipers ever struck from behind during 'The Road To The Isles'? Had a carelessly tossed caber ever brought the under-elevens' Highland dancing to a tragically premature halt? It turned out the man I was talking to was not only a caber tosser himself but a railwayman, who worked on the line to Kyle of Lochalsh. He assured me that the last eighty miles of my journey would in no way be an anti-climax. He was right, and if anything he underestimated its impact.

The first few miles to Dingwall run alonside Moray Firth, and across the water a peninsula forbiddingly called the Black Isle catches the attention. It looks rather pleasant and fertile to me and it turns out it's only called the Black Isle because it is sheltered and relatively warm in winter, so that when the surrounding area is white with snow, the 'Isle' remains black. This was one of the many titbits of information about the Skye Line (as they call the line from Dingwall to the Kyle) that I gleaned from a very hardworking British Rail guide who travels in an 1897 restaurant coach, converted into an observation car and attached to these trains during the summer. For a small surcharge you can sit in an armchair and gaze out at some of the most dramatic views in Scotland and learn about Raven Rock and the Valley of Drizzle and all the other names that make this line sound, as well as look, as if it belongs in the pages of Tolkien.

There is an air of gloomy beauty to the landscape as the train cuts across Scotland from the North Sea to the Atlantic. It's early summer and the

17.45 to Kyle of Lochalsh is almost full today, but I should imagine it's a lonely line in winter. This is borne out when I chat to a level-crossing keeper near Strathcarron. He's a southerner, an ex-academic who came to this lonely crossing to get away from it all. He claims that one day in deepest winter he overslept and was woken by the sound of an approaching train. He put duty before modesty and leapt out on to the crossing and flung the doors open stark naked. He's philosophical about the railway up here. I asked him if he was alarmed when one year a train failed to stop and ploughed through both the gates. 'Oh, heavens no . . . it kept us in firewood all winter.'

The last ten miles of the line from Stromeferry to Kyle of Lochalsh curve tortuously by the side of Loch Carron, providing a spectacular grand finale on a three-hour journey that has already been a heady entertainment of constantly changing landscapes. The rock through which the train wends its way is some of the oldest in the world and it took four years to push the line these last ten miles, at a cost of over £20,000 a mile. Some thirty-one rock cuttings were blasted out and twenty-nine bridges were built and when they finally reached the end of the stubborn peninsula in 1896 they had to blast out the foundations for the Kyle of Lochalsh terminus itself. The government of the day had provided a grant of £45,000 to support the fish and mail trades which it was hoped would make these epic efforts of engineering worthwhile, but it seems that the Kyle never prospered and expanded in the way they'd all expected, and in 1971, final consent was given to its closure (Scotland having already lost nearly 4000 miles of its 7391 miles of railway between 1950 and 1972). But the locals fought such a vigorous campaign in defence of their line that people from all over Britain became aware of it for the first time, passenger traffic increased, and the oil discoveries on the West Coast became a decisive factor in a change of mind by the government in 1974.

So, a journey from Euston to the Isle of Skye is still possible. Mine had taken me over 785 miles of railway, and it was drizzling as our Class 27 diesel drew its five-coach load into Kyle Station and came to a halt with a discreet hiss, its snub yellow nose facing the rising bulk of the Isle of Skye across a thin strip of sea. Skye was dark and mysterious and silent. A wisp of low cloud straggled across its mountain tops.

I said goodbye to my travelling companions – a bright-eyed ninety-nine-year-old called Jean MacKenzie who'd travelled this line as a young girl in 1897, the year it opened, two Danish students who had come to learn

Kyle of Lochalsh station, and beyond it, the Isle of Skye

English and who already spoke it better than anyone else on the train, especially the English, and two Americans – a Texan girl who'd never been near a train in the States and a flavor chemist from the mid-west called Constantine Apostle who had brought his bicycle all the way from Chicago to Scotland for a holiday. We had chatted in comfortable, relaxed fashion in the way one only does on trains.

I was sad to leave them and sad to feel that I had reached the end of a journey which I never thought I would ever make – the length of Britain by rail. It goes without saying that I would recommend it to anyone, not only for the sixty-four pure malt whiskies that faced me that last evening at the excellent Lochalsh Hotel, but also for the 565 miles of railway travel back south down the magnificent West Highland Line to Glasgow and London, which will cure any hangover.

THE TRAIN-SPOTTER IN 1980

I was a hopeless case in the first place. There was no question of converting me to railways. For me there is little in transport to rival the sensation of racing, unhampered through city and country alike. In my experience trains are late no more often than planes are delayed or cars caught in heavy traffic. You don't have to leave the ground, you don't have to have a sick-bag in the seat in front of you, you don't have to change a wheel in fog on a motorway. You can read, you can smoke, you can lounge, you can lean, you can stare out of the window or go for a walk, and with a little luck you can eat and drink something whilst so doing. Rail travel is also probably better for your heart and figures show it's certainly better for other parts of your body as well; your chances of being in an accident on a rail journey are 200 times less than they are on a car journey. But the railways very often fail to live up to their potential. The commuter services around London for instance move many of their passengers in crowded, cramped, filthy, out-of-date stock. High Speed Train travel is a poor joke to people whose misfortune it is to find themselves on some of British Rail's cross-country services – from Glasgow to Manchester or Bristol to Newcastle, for instance – where the rolling stock is old and shabby and the overworked diesels fail with monotonous regularity, and the buffet's closed because no staff have turned up.

But no one *wants* to run a railway like this, it's just the result of a reluctance on the part of successive governments, both Labour and Conservative, to realise and wholeheartedly to commit themselves to extensive investment in one of the most sane and sensible and cost-effective ways of moving people and materials around the country. The German and the French governments have realised this; even the Americans, whose railroads seemed destined for total extinction a few years ago, are now reorganising and experiencing increasing demand for this potentially most civilised form of travel. I would rather the government spent my money on the tangible benefits of a fast, clean, efficient railway network which carries over a million passengers a day, than, for instance, £123 million annually on Concorde which carries 100,000 passengers a year.

On my journey to the Kyle I met drivers and stationmasters and stationmistresses and signalmen and everywhere I was impressed by the commitment to running a national railway system despite a chronic and persistent and demoralising shortage of money. The engineering skill and the human effort is all there ready and waiting for a government sane enough to use it. Although it's twenty-five years since I nearly burst blood vessels trying to see the Thames–Clyde Express, I feel now more than ever that it's important to get excited about railways. Try going from Euston to Kyle of Lochalsh. Then I think you'll see what I mean.

EUROPE

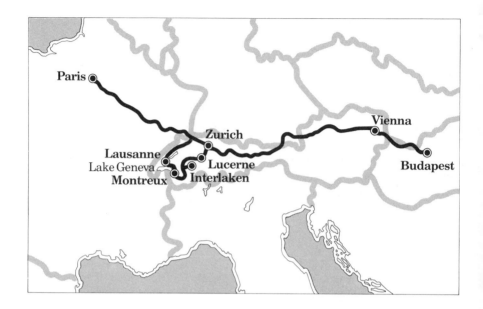

Changing Trains

ERIC ROBSON

My journey really began thirty years ago.

I remember it was a summer afternoon, the sort that never seem to happen after you're ten years old. Roses on a rural station platform buzzed with life. The sounds of cattle lazing in warm grass tumbled from the hill and beside me crouched another animal – a blue metallic beast panting slightly from its exertions.

It was big; so big it even dwarfed my grandfather the stationmaster. With a struggle he lifted this fat four-year-old above the wheels and the engine man's broad hands reached down to carry me over the metal threshold. And here was something better than the wind-up tractor I got for Christmas. A grotto of gleaming pipes and whispering gauges.

'So you'd like to drive it?'

That's all he said. The routine, solitary line of conversation with which this strong man had captured the imagination of a thousand little boys.

The shovel scraped, the firebox flashed its glow across the floor, wheels pounded like an athlete flexing before a race and I was back on the platform watching *Mallard* lead its brood of clackety coaches away into Scotland.

It must have lasted all of five minutes, and yet that locomotive had breathed on me. The scent of warm oil and swirling soot lingered.

In later years when railways ran me to work and drove me to distraction it was still there. While the chances of getting to an appointment on time ticked away in a slummy siding in Crewe or the digestive system protested the lack of a buffet car between London and Newcastle, the smell would occasionally drift across the compartment – I swear as tangible as the aroma in an 'Ah, Bisto' advert.

I smelled it a moment ago too, wrapped in the steam of fresh coffee. I'm waiting for another train, this time in a platform-side café of the Paris Gare de Lyon. My journey's taking me into another world of railways. Down the great lines of Europe where past glories are remembered every bit as fondly as they are in the breast of the pioneering British. But which way to go? The choice is Milan or south to Marseilles. The east perhaps, in the track of the Stamboul train. Certainly nowhere by the direct route. I've got a week to travel, a week of changing trains and stopping where I like.

I wonder where these people are going and would like to go? The grumpy and the glazed. Commuters you could transfer to any one of a dozen cities and who, at this time of the morning, probably wouldn't notice if you did. The worriers. Whiskered old men and out of town scholars; Germans on business and newly fledged soldiers. The middle-age ladies that make every Frenchman dream of home, wearing flour bags as if they're the latest creation by Cardin. (If indeed they're not.) And girls with empty eyes and open mouths parading their A level in mascara application. All with heads tilted up to the indicator boards and lost in their own adventures.

'Trans Europe Express. Le Cisalpin . . .'

The station announcer makes the decision for me. A ticket, a hurried reservation and a jostle through the crowd brings me face to face with the hostess in blue. My slightly sweaty handshake is rewarded by a smile that could melt a ticket collector at Euston.

'You speak English monsieur.'

She must know from the state of my palms.

'Carriage 16 seat 21. May you have a delightful trip monsieur.'

After such a welcome I'm sure I could turn a blind eye to any faults – even if they've forgotten to couple up the dining car or if they park us in the French equivalent of Crewe. But then of course those things don't happen on Trans Europe Express. These are the better than first-class continental trains, the internationalist's dream, running across the frontiers of a dozen countries in much the same way that the luxury expresses of the Wagons Lits Company did a hundred years before them.

We leave with a hiss of air conditioning. There are four and a half hours in which to bask in luxury seating and sample the other delights of this aluminium tube before the first destination on Lake Geneva.

Ten kilometres gone and the train is a grey snake on a grey landscape. Mist reaches up to the windows. Twenty kilometres and the first surreptitious glances at fellow travellers.

They're certainly not the élite bunch we'd have journeyed with a century ago. By the look of it not a middle European king or end of the line archduchess amongst them. Neither do they seem to be the breed of spies and arms dealers that used to shuttle back and forth to the Balkans and, according to the story books, kept the Orient Expresses in business. No, I fear they're just the routine traffic of our more mundane multinational business.

Mind you, we're in debt to those early trains – the privileged expresses that extended the privilege of travel to the rest of us. Before them we were bound in by the narrow circles of our city or village life. Then the railway tracks went over the horizon.

'Prendre Le Crampton.'

A strange approach in any circumstances.

'You've not heard of Le Crampton?' At first I suspect that the French passenger in the double-breasted suit across the gangway is being suggestive in a gallic sort of way. It turns out that Monsieur Charbonnier ('You won't know me' . . . I didn't, 'but you will have heard of the cars I sell' . . . I had) is jolly bored because he travels this way a lot.

'Prendre Le Crampton, we sometimes say, meaning catch the train.'

'Oh, I see.' (Which I didn't.)

'It should make you feel at home here. Cramptons were English locomotives we used to pull express trains. From Bristol I think they came but I'm not sure. They had wheels – you say *énorme*. I remember from seeing pictures of them. Something we owe England.'

'Something,' said with just a hint of malice I feel. But I'm spared. Monsieur Charbonnier is by now bored with this conversation and settling on a lady in the next patch. How do you say it – a butterfly *énorme*. Thirty kilometres and I'm being bitchily British already.

The Times crossword, like a horoscope uncannily appropriate whatever the circumstances, offers as a clue: 2 down, Tender of material for French railways, 5 letters.

The sun sucks away the last layer of mist and we're running beside the reflections of the River Yonne. Barges at Sens, the tiny inland harbour at Laroche, Tonnerre with its name sparkling in flowers on the platform.

I squeeze past Monsieur Charbonnier, by now bestowing his five sentences on someone else, and explore the train. In the burnished buffet car the barside haggling is just a high-speed version of the conversation in any Paris café. Only the pinball machine is missing. They haven't forgotten the dining car though; it's a bubble of excellence rolling through French farmyards. Not all the early delights of train travel have gone, it seems. Here you can still nibble at the pleasures which were once the prerogative of the rich and famous. In the best traditions of the Wagon Lits service that made those first expresses the fashionable way to travel, the waiters still get by in three or four languages. With the politeness of men who know they're the best at their job they assume that we recognise the dishes on today's menu as old friends but they're still prepared to discuss with a quiet American what's the next best thing to Californian claret.

Serving trays dressed with tiny roses bring a first course of Darne de Colin Hôtelière. Later, Navarin d'Agneau Printanier. Wine, liqueurs and a growing sympathy for the poor souls 30,000 feet above us who are having their digestive fires damped by a layer of airline plastic 'food'.

The train stops. It's the first border – between France and Switzerland. The formalities at Vallorbe are accomplished with an efficiency born of a hundred years of practice. Seven minutes later the customs and immigration men are aboard, the engine has been changed and we're on our way.

But there's a flaw in this comfortable system. These Trans Europe expresses were a vision of the fifties. They were going to unite Europe as never before, using the same high-speed trains everywhere, taking bookings through a central computer. They've already failed. The locomotives may be all-electric but there are still four different voltages in use in Europe. The network which is controlled by a different country every four years hasn't been able to agree on the type of service to offer or even something as simple as the colour of its trains. The railways are as nationalist a business now as they were when the elegant staff of the Orient expresses smoothed the unfamiliar business of passport control.

Soon perhaps Le Cisalpin will be as out of place and time as those first great trains and the luxurious European resorts the railways created. Soon this arrival through the suburbs of Lausanne could be no more than a picture for someone's scrapbook.

'La jeune génération a besoin de héros.'

A slogan dripped in aerosol red on a bank window across the street from Lausanne main station. The need is greater now than when the twin towns of Lausanne and Montreux were at the height of their popularity. Then they and their visitors were self-assured, wealthy and fashionable. This corner of Switzerland on the shores of the Lake of Geneva was little England in the season. The well-to-do came here to take the Alpine air and be pampered in hotels that had almost as many stars as they had servants.

The greatest of them, the Montreux Palace, is still in business. You can still take the long walk through its music room and lounges, past the salon de bridge and out on to a balcony that traps the sunset. The brochures don't mention the customers though. Tonight a sales conference for Chevrolet. Clean-cut young Americans, all badges and company ties, their wives and girlfriends outdoing each other in evening frocks that somehow all manage to include the company colours.

'Gee!' (A word apparently not confined to Superman comics.) 'You'd better believe the time we're going to have when we hit Seattle.' Others in the company are planning to be equally aggressive in Chicago, Detroit and Los Angeles. The common front begins to disintegrate when the conversation turns to local sightseeing. 'That château at Chillon, wasn't that just beautiful,' asserts a lady with go-faster stripes. A man rattling a glass of bourbon grumbles that it just looked like a slice of rockpile to him. I head for the bar.

Later the barman points out the young ladies from the casino who are hard at work looking pretty. He gives me a run down of their respective prices much to the embarrassment of the clean-cut young men who are with them. The gentlemen who used to come here would be appalled at such goings on, or perhaps they'd just be amazed that the cost of living has gone up so much.

The rack-and-pinion railway takes tourists from Montreux up to the ski slopes of Rochers de Naye above Lake Geneva

In the best traditions of *News of the World* reporters I make an excuse and leave. I have an early start tomorrow.

Early and cold.

A single speck of blue on a white sheet, the electric railcar is tacking up the mountain above Montreux. There are 6700 feet to the ski slopes of Rochers de Naye. The scenery that tempted us has disappeared behind a swirl of snow and steamy, running windows. The passengers, mainly dogs and sportsmen, are breathing with gusto as they jump out at little stations along the way. Skiers, pets, baggage and all are dumped in a snowdrift apparently in the middle of nowhere. We plough on, the driver and I, until we reach the relative comfort of a basement railway terminus under the hotel at the summit. A ten-minute stop and a cigarette in defiance of the spirit of fitness that's occupied the train for the last hour; then with a nipped nose, powdery snow in my hair and feet that are quite wet enough

I'm back on board. The driver changes ends and the train begins to feel its way backwards out into the worsening weather. A vague sound of clockwork under the floor presumably means that the cog-wheel is finding its interlocking teeth in the rack under the snow, but looking ahead there's just a single, fragile, overhead wire and it looks for all the world as if our tiny carriage is using it to navigate a precarious course through the boarded tunnels and ice forests that lie between us and the sunshine of Lake Geneva.

Below the snowline and through the trees, away across the valley, there's a sudden plume of smoke and the unmistakable whistle of steam trains at work. The call to breakfast.

The kitchen is a log cabin behind the engine shed. Men and boys in an odd assortment of engine drivers' hats are drying socks and warming fingers. From first light when they'd shivered out of their bunk beds in the converted railway carriages down the line they've been coaling and polishing, working harder than anybody being paid for the job would even consider. But then these are the volunteers of the Blonay Chamby line, welding, greasing or navvying for fun, every day they can steal away from school or their real job.

This used to be one of a hundred rural steam railways but now it's the last of them, in this part of Switzerland at least. It's a reservation in the hills above Montreux where the railway of the old days is preserved in axle grease to fire the imagination of a new type of traveller.

Feet are crammed into railway boots, cups with memories of Ffestiniog or Stockton and Darlington are rattled into the sink and the part-timers of Blonay Chamby rush off to prepare for the morning invasion. Down the line comes the first excursion of the day, which has a touch of Bangladesh about it, so many bodies and bits of bodies protrude from every available hole.

These visitors are somewhat different from milords and ladies who used to come here. For one thing they actually want to get close to the machines that frighten the horses. No sooner has the little train stopped than an avalanche of photographic hardware covers the track. Whooping and shuttering like some plague of space-age locusts they set about devouring every nameplate and return valve, all the while gibbering to each other about 'rack tanks' and '0-4-0s'.

I've stumbled across a colony of that peculiarly British species, the greater trainspotter, in one of its annual migrations. They've gone up-

The Panoramic Express of the Montreux–Oberland–Bernoise Railway near Gstaad

market since my day when the hobby was limited to hanging off a railway bridge in Carlisle, getting generally filthy, but at the end of the day proudly underlining *City of Glasgow* or *Sir Nigel Gresley*, two new locomotives captured for the collection. Now they flit across the world to mop up the railways of Indonesia or the USA, to ride the last steam service in one corner of South Africa or to photograph a famous haul on the Indian railroad. It's all part of the package holiday business now, a thriving trade designed to cater for older schoolboys who had withdrawal symptoms when British Rail were silly enough to get rid of their steam trains, and who for choice would still have *Rocket* at the head of the Liverpool – Manchester inter-city services.

Beam me up Dr Spock.

You see, that's the beauty of a journey like this. It's mainly a journey of the imagination through a world of railways that, let's face it, has already gone. Even if you don't find the actual engines you can still feel what life was like when they came this way. You don't have to touch the firebox or

The Blonay Chamby line; the museum railway crosses the only viaduct on this scenic route

stand on a footplate to appreciate the spirit of enterprise and confidence that the railways carried with them.

For example, you could stand here at the end of the Blonay Chamby line in the early thirties and watch a very special train go by. While much of Europe was closing its doors against the cold wind of depression, the pioneers of railway luxury were still backing their hunches.

The Pullman company, determined to break into the European market which was dominated by Wagons Lits, built the only narrow-gauge pullman train in the world. The Golden Mountain Pullman would have passed us here in 1931, an electric train just out of its box, taking corners like a Hornby model on its way to the smarter ski resorts of the Bernese

Oberland. The luxury of the main lines had found its way off the beaten track.

Today's train is something special too, a miniature blue train, double-headed for the climb over the Golden Pass. In two hours the wide-screen windows of the Panoramic Express take us from the B feature of the lower slopes to the main attraction. A field of mountain tops under a deep blue cover. On the way up each twist through the trees brings a new postcard impression. Up through sheer vineyards, mist in layers below and the surface of Lake Geneva a strange, upside-down sky. At La Tine a power station, with one of the best views in the world; railway sheds at Châteaux d'Oex disguised as chalets. And everywhere wooden houses leaning over the line, carved and colourful. 'Home is the sailor, home from the sea and the hunter home from the hill' chipped above a door in Gstaad, a welcome to the generations of tourists who inspired this railway and are still its best customers.

The private, narrow-gauge Montreux–Oberland–Bernoise railway has made its living since the turn of the century by bringing trippers round the mountain. Their train drops from the high pass, round an impossible postage-stamp airfield and into the station at Zweisimmen. Everyone changes to the less panoramic rolling stock of the private but this time standard-gauge Bern–Lotschberg–Simplon railway. It's just across the platform and about to leave for the hour-long haul to Interlaken.

This is certainly not the route for people who object to changing trains. You could take any one of a hundred journeys across Switzerland and never have to use the same company twice. Each one of them has its own company pride and canton affiliations. They're the people's railways every bit as much as the great systems that have the official stamp of state ownership.

The tolling bells of the level crossings are echoed by cow bells on the mountains as we roll through orchards of marzipan apples into Interlaken. Here's a railway town that spoils you for choice, with seven or eight liveries touting to take you up, over or through the mountains. Switzerland's just a giant train set really where generations of fathers and sons have added more track and extra trains whenever it's taken their fancy. With the single-mindedness of men who've made railways their hobby the Swiss are even prepared to pay for them when they lose money, subsidising the private companies to allow them to carry on giving a community service. And anyway, in a nation suffering from referendum disease of epidemic proportions it's virtually impossible to get agreement to close them. Dr Beeching would have had a rough ride in Switzerland. Mind you, the private companies don't have the layout entirely to themselves. There is a proper state system as well which is going to provide my fourth train of the day.

The dull, green locomotive of Swiss Federal Railways' only narrow-gauge line roars eastwards round the hem of the Jungfrau. This is the Switzerland of the less energetic Victorians. Not the high Alps but the fringe of the mountains. A view of the snow from the comfort of a travelling rug and a good book. Occasionally they would look up from the pages of the latest thriller.

'Over there, dear, that's the falls at Meiringen. You remember, where Sherlock Holmes had his nastiest encounter.'

I never liked Conan Doyle and the falls aren't much to write home about either, if they're to be judged by the view from the carriage. The train gives an extra rumble and we're climbing. Not relying on legs, too steep for ordinary wheels. We're on the rack – a painfully slow twenty miles an hour as the cogs under the engine and carriages wind us more than 3000 feet to the top of the Brunig pass. It's an up and over railway with no more than a moment's silent running at the summit before we're plunging into the one in ten or one in twelve gradients that will bring us to the shore of the Lake of the four forest Cantons and a night in Lucerne. I'd better make the most of it because there's a stiffer climb tomorrow.

It's an odd light, a reflection of the purple ring of mountains, that bathes this turreted lakeside terminus at Vitznau across the water from Lucerne. A white steamer has just come and gone dropping a solitary passenger and a few boxes of greengroceries. A railwayman pushes the single goods wagon round on the turntable and hitches it to the train. The early morning 'up goods' is about to climb out of the station. This is the milk round, the brewery dray and the fruit and veg van all rolled into one for the people who live without a road on Rigi Mountain. It's the school bus and at the other end of a life the ambulance and hearse. It's picturesque with its tiny red electric engine. It's quaint in that it stops at each house on the way. But the Vitznau Rigi Bahn doesn't survive for any reason of sentiment. I'm travelling on a mountain lifeline that's been getting the mails and supplies through without fail since 21 May 1871 when in the depths of the Franco-Prussian war it was opened as Europe's first mountain railway.

The Vitznau Rigi and the Arth Rigi race down parallel tracks just before they diverge

You need a head for heights. When Mark Twain travelled this way in the little train that seems to lean out over the precipice on the corners, he felt that the one in five gradients provided a good opportunity for remembering his sins and repenting of them. Getting safely to Freibergen halfway up the mountain is a cause for celebration, a moment to ease the cramp in white knuckles. They're quite used to foreigners staggering off the train and asking for a drink because Rigi is a special occasions railway as well.

In an engine house that looks like something out of the wild west steam engines from the 1920s are polished to perfection. Black, crouching locomotives, built with sloping bodies so that the boilers work on the mountain inclines, are brought out in the summer to pull the party trains.

In decked-out open carriages, with accordion music drowning out the strains of hard-working steam, they come here to celebrate an engagement or toast a bride. The Japanese are among the regular party customers, slapping leather thighs and yahooing with the best of them. But mainly it's still the Swiss themselves having an ethnic knees up while congratulating themselves for having the nous to hang on to railways that other less sensible nations would have 'rationalised' a generation ago.

And after the party there isn't a better hangover cure than the wind in your face at the summit. To get to the bottom of the mountain in Switzerland – you've probably already guessed – I use a different railway, operated by a separate company on the other side. The Arth Goldau Rigi Bahn may look like a pokey local train but because the Swiss take everything, and particularly railways, with the utmost seriousness it still connects at the bottom with the federal main-line expresses to Zurich.

It is 7 a.m. and the hangover's still there, which only goes to prove that the wind in the face on mountain tops isn't all it's cracked up to be. But there's something reassuring about railway stations at this time of the morning. The victory of timetable efficiency over human weakness. We may not be sufficiently awake to know what day of the week it is but the railway has already been up and about for hours. Whilst I'm still marvelling at the strength of stomach that enables these strange Europeans to eat salami and drink schnapps at breakfast my train's already been dressed for the day. Washed, stocked and shuffled into the right position in the pack of 1000 trains that are dealt out across the continent every day from Zurich.

Of course everything should run smoothly here. They've had enough practice after all. Since the very first departure of transcontinental railways Switzerland has been the turntable of Europe. When the Swiss are being very 'British' and refuse to bring their clocks into line with the rest of their neighbours, the ripple of resulting chaos runs through the timetables of half a dozen countries. Whether you're travelling west to east like me or north to south you can scarcely avoid using Switzerland as a staging-post.

As a result Swiss railwaymen still consider themselves to be engaged on work of national importance. Like the railwaymen of India that are still manning an outpost of empire, drivers and guards here have retained their status in the eyes of the community long after the initial prestige of railways died. They are men with authority and a uniform to prove it.

Departure. To the Swiss a moment of religious observance. It would of course be a sin if the train was late. I'm aboard the Transalpin for the longest part of this journey – ten hours to Vienna in a train even more comfortable than the Trans-Europe Cisalpin that brought me out of Paris. An orange express in the livery of Austrian State Railways and simply the best train

The Transalpin, the most luxurious train of the Austrian railway network

that the Osterreichischen Bundesbahnen has to offer; the star of this single main line to the east.

After the Austrian passport formalities at Buchs the first hours are devoted to the scenery and the flickering pictures of lineside life. At Murg the stationmaster's wife is hanging her sheets to dry in the station waiting-room; fields of maize are marching up to the line in impeccable formation; the corn is stacked in sheaves like shadowy arab women walking across a bare meadow. Above it all the sweep of the Tyrol and an occasional bulbous spire stubbing above the trees to give away the presence of another village and another change of scene.

Then the train turns in on itself. It begins to take on the feeling of a not unpleasant seventy-mile-an-hour hotel. There are all the same advantages – a captive audience, people to overhear, anonymity if you want it. Along the corridor there's a public telephone (that works) and every so often there's a visit from the manager to check that we're enjoying our stay.

The Transalpin thunders through Jenbach, an obscure, rusty siding. From the main-line express you may catch a glimpse of a little steam engine

The Zillertahlbahn takes the traveller into a world of steam trains that has remained unchanged since the 1920s

heading for the hills. That's all you'll see. But if you were to stop and climb aboard the Zillertahlbahn you could travel into a world of railways that's scarcely changed since the 1920s. It's a line straight out of the pages of one of the Reverend Awdry's books. As the tiny train plods along the valley floor you expect to see round each bend the fat controller or, at the very least, Thomas the tank engine.

But it's no childish dream. For the people who live and work between the main line and its terminus at Mayerhofen the Ziller, as it's known to Europe's railway enthusiasts, is an important as any Trans-Europe service. Freight to the local factories is transferred on special bogies that lift whole trains off the Austrian State Railways and on to its two-feet gauge private track. And unlike its nationalised neighbour that needs millions of Schillings in subsidy every year, this line just about breaks even with a little help from volunteers and tourists.

It's tempting to stay. But then, even though the Ziller is a gem, it doesn't have proper steam engines – you know, big ones on main-line trains. I'll have to travel a lot further to find them.

A waiter with polished heels clicks to attention and offers the services of the dining car for lunch. I'm sharing a table with two English double-glazing salesmen who proceed to try to dismantle their demonstration model window using the train cutlery. The manager is not amused.

'Where are you going?' It's the salesman with the bent knife that speaks.

'I don't know.'

He glances up at me to check for further signs of mental deficiency.

'Well, why are you travelling this way?'

'I'm just enjoying the journey.'

'Work, is it?' Bent fork chips in, having summoned up his best technique for dealing with difficult customers.

'I just enjoy train journeys.'

There's silence for the rest of the meal apart from the clicking or snapping of knives and forks.

I doze by a window and think off the effects of lunch. Past churchyards with their leaning wrought-iron crosses and coloured portraits of the dead. Nameless stations and abandoned halts. Here a wooden shack slumped across the platform. There elder trees growing through a booking hall. At a level crossing a solitary cyclist under a cloud of flies and in the ruins of an engine shed an upturned wooden sledge. I imagine it was the 'Rosebud' of a railway magnate. Sleep.

'Innsbruck. We are now arriving at Innsbruck,' says the girl on the loudspeaker. The platform signs say Vienna. It was a good idea to get Austrian television to record the in-train announcements on cassettes – so long as you put the cassettes in the right order. We've arrived at Innsbruck three times on this trip which is particularly unnerving for sleepy passengers like me.

But it's everything we expected Vienna to be. Good food and tasteful music. The sounds of a string quintet drifting across the tables. I close my eyes and soak up the atmosphere of a little restaurant up in the woods somewhere. Except it's really the station caff. You won't find many railway pie jokes on the Westbahnhof. The chunk of marble that's Vienna West station is more than somewhere to depart from as quickly as possible. It's a place to eat and meet by choice rather than necessity. It's where I met a colleague, one of that corps of foreign correspondents that sit in Vienna with an ear pressed to the wall of the eastern bloc.

'There are two types of train in Austria,' he tells me, 'the Transalpin and the rest. If you're unfortunate enough to be travelling on the rest you've

One of Austria's last main-line steam locomotives

got a choice of slow trains and even slower trains. They call them all expresses.'

He rummages in the recesses of his sports jacket and brings out a handful of tickets. 'There's the problem.' Ten bits of cardboard fall on to the table, the tickets for a 200-mile journey. 'You see they never managed to get rid of the Franz Joseph mentality. The bureaucrats in the outer office are still trying to make the place run as slowly as possible.' The cynicism that's bound to come if you spend your life listening at walls.

Once you could have sat here and looked out from the platforms of the old Westbahnhof to see that this was not a place of happy meetings. The trains still came as if life in Vienna was running on schedule. The Nazi Orient Express brought officials of the high command, and the next train to arrive on platform two carried the red star of occupation on its smokebox door. Whoever came, the people of Vienna still died in the streets and the old world of pre-war railways died too in the ruins of the Austro-Hungarian Empire.

The survivors of Europe put on a new face. There were new appointments to keep. But the old, prestige expresses would no longer carry people to them. They were symbols of an age we wanted to forget. It's only with the distortion of memory that we pretend they could have survived.

Against the odds bits of them do. There's even a remnant of the Orient Express. A fallen woman of a train now, a grubby daily to Bucharest that hardly justifies the honour of being called an express. Once the most capitalist of trains it's now had its name pinched to boost business on a cheap run to Rumania.

But if you want to see the real prestige of European railways today you have to walk away from the station and stand for a moment on the edge of the Vienna freight yards. This is the modern business that's taken over the lines which once echoed to first-class passenger traffic. This is where profits grease the sliding away of national frontiers. Here today, Hull tomorrow in a roundabout of heavy haulage that notches up one small advance in the battle with the airlines. People are just not as profitable as containers.

E.R.I.C. . . . R.O.B. . . . I've never been able to resist those machines on stations that punch out your name on little metal strips. They still have them in the Vienna Sudbahnhof among the glass cases of model trains that are the Austrian passion. My colleague the correspondent was grumbling that he can't get served in his local shop because of middle-aged modellers agonising over what coupling they should use or which new piece of rolling stock to buy. Suddenly the station is full of bleary-eyed young men trying desperately hard to be rowdy. They're the green army, football supporters of the S. C. Rapid team, off on manoeuvres. They barge through the ticket gate jeering at other passengers and jostling the collector. It makes me feel quite homesick.

In a distant corner of the Sudbahnhof a very special passenger train is arriving. The Chopin express is a train for poor people, known here as the emigrant train. Arriving at dawn each day from Moscow it carries among its passengers the flotsam of political repression. The platform is piled high with battered suitcases and broken boxes; among the luggage little scenes from other people's lives, tears and long-held embraces. These are families and bits of families that count themselves lucky to have got the exit visa which allows them a sort of freedom after perhaps years of struggle. For these people Vienna is the neutral stronghold where the struggle stops.

My journey is to the fringes of the world they've left behind. Five days out from London I'm going to raise a corner of their curtain and slip across the border into Hungary. It's a nervous moment. Will it be as sininster as preconceptions and imagination would have us believe? Is it significant that the Lehar Express is my thirteenth train? An hour from Vienna it rolls into the border checkpoint of Hegyesalom, sending up a flight of pigeons as it groans to a halt beside a peeling and dusty station forecourt. The wire fence that's been guarding the train for the last few kilometres is suddenly rustier.

Little groups of armed soldiers stand about. I'm reminded that people were shot on this frontier not many weeks before. The train is taken over by an army of workmen, tapping wheels, climbing over bogies and, in the carriages, peering into ceiling cavities and shining torches under the seats. My passport is checked four times and finally stamped with a multi-coloured seal of approval. A girl scuttling about the compartments with an official briefcase demands to know if I have Hungarian money, and scuttles away again before I have a chance to answer.

There's a jolt that sends the most formal of the passport guards reeling into a spare seat. The Locomotive and dining car of Magyar Alamvasutak have apparently arrived. The soldiers haven't found a spy or an illegal immigrant today but then they probably hardly ever do. In half an hour we're on our way tracking the Danube through the flat landscape of the Northern Plain of Hungary. It's three hours to Budapest.

I walk along for breakfast to be ignored by a waiter with a serious face, black suit and incongruous Afro hairstyle. Apparently he's not pleased that I've stopped at the kitchen door to admire the coal-fired range. I'm hungry enough to polish off the pork and chips but the coarse Czecho-slovak pils is really too much for this time of morning.

Through grubby windows is the poor end of the Austro-Hungarian empire. Fought over and bartered in a score of European conflicts, in the last war it was levelled in punishment for not knowing what side it was on. And always these railways were destroyed because military men, at least, know how important they are. The train, slow at the best of times, slows still further to negotiate sections that are being rebuilt. That's been a protracted business because Hungary had little help. Its new masters had long memories and saw the advantages of a generation of poverty. But eventually as this line proves business sense prevailed. They didn't have to like the west to trade with it, and trade needs trade routes, the access to markets that new railways through Hungary can provide.

It's by no means a one-way traffic. On the Lehar express I'm surrounded by groups of Austrian women out on a shopping spree, gossiping their way to Budapest where they can buy food cheaper than at home. The story goes that the Viennese travelled on this train to buy their Viennese sausage at cut price. Families have shared Vienna and Budapest ever since the old, extravagant days of Austro-Hungary and it will take more than a new line on the map to break the habit. Eventually the Hungarian government gave in and Austrians no longer need a visa to come here.

We arrive at Budapest through a back door of poor industrial suburbs that lead you to expect an eastern European equivalent of Wigan North Western rather than the ceremonial arch of Keleti station. The shoppers throw themselves and me off the train and all my illusions of life behind the iron curtain fall to pieces as I'm pushed into the path of a girl in a John Travolta T shirt who disappears into an espresso coffee shop that's advertising Coca Cola and hot dogs. The hand of state enterprise apparently can't conceal the fact that this is basically a capitalist city.

Later, after the taxi driver had practised his own version of the free market economy on me by charging three times the rate, there's a view in the pink evening light of the twin cities of Buda and Pest from the balcony of the hotel. The very hotel where Zaharoff the arms dealer, newly arrived off the Orient Express, conducted his shadowy business. In the lounge the Czarda orchestra, a musical bridge to the passions of Hungary's past, tonight mutilates 'Scotland the Brave' in honour of their foreign visitor.

Outside it's beginning to rain as I set off to a corner of the city I've been determined to visit. Over the bridge and past the brighter shopping streets the pavements eventually give way to potholes, the fine riverside houses to broken, unpainted fencing. Two miles perhaps, in a street of shuttered warehouses and peeling bungalows. And then I find them. By the roadside among the trees the remains of Hungary's railway heritage. Line upon line of derelict locomotives, the grass high and thick through the wheels. Chalk messages scrawled on rusty metal; the occasional creak of an iron door. Dead. And yet they still have that smell about them, the oil and soot stirred by a shower of rain.

Railways in Hungary as in the rest of Europe have turned their back on steam trains in the same way that they've outgrown the financiers who

conceived them. Railways, first designed to extend the power of powerful men, became the great levellers. A socialist ideal. You can visit the nursery of that ideal in a forest overlooking Budapest.

A red and yellow diesel locomotive has arrived at the head of a crowded excursion train. Its passengers are adults but the guards and porters are children. If they work hard at school they can do a shift on the Pioneer railway and learn to be the railway persons of the future. In this society, too, it's important to know how to run the trains on time. With the train crew in the canteen, eating sticky cakes and drinking lemonade, 'I'm told how important trains will be in the future. 'When we put down our new tracks and get the new engines,' says a fourteen-year-old, 'the railways will be so different and so modern you won't recognise them.'

Perhaps I'm already too late. But if there's just a chance of seeing that generation of working steam I've come so far to find I'll travel on.

The tracks lead towards another frontier as I follow the retreating steam eastwards. At every stop there are railwaymen who lean on booking-office counters, shake their heads and tell stories of the trains that used to run and the steam engines that were here just a week before. Then suddenly, on a reservation up near the border with Czechoslovakia, there they are; dinosaurs grazing. Beasts from the mythology of railways that are still a potent reminder of past endeavours. No main-line train is entrusted to these steam locomotives now. They'll shunt freight into a brief twilight and then be left to grow cold.

It will fall to the enginemen of Hungary to damp down the fires of European main-line steam, but when they do it will be with the same conflicting emotions as men of the breed in Doncaster or Crewe.

The grass is knee-high where a signal box once stood. I pick my way through the rubble of station buildings. A few discarded bolts are all that remain of the line. It's thirty years since I first stood on this platform. During these years railways had to find a new job for themselves. They had to change or die. Some died anyway. Now out of the factories come trains that like intercontinental jets put real speed into travel and take every other scrap of pleasure out. Soon perhaps we'll long for a reminder of today's gentle expresses. But then it won't be so bad. Whatever happens to the trains we can still use our imagination.

Among the sounds of a summer afternoon isn't that *Mallard* we can hear away down the valley?

A derelict locomotive in the
railway graveyard at Budapest

NOTES
ON THE CONTRIBUTORS

MICHAEL FRAYN has published five novels—*The Tin Men, The Russian Interpreter, Towards the End of the Morning, A Very Private Life* and *Sweet Dreams.* His plays include *The Two of Us, The Sandboy, Alphabetical Order,* which won the *Evening Standard* Best Comedy Award, and *Donkey's Years,* which won the Society of West End Theatres Award for Comedy of the Year, *Clouds* and *Liberty Hall.* In 1980 *Make and Break* opened at the Lyric Theatre, transferred to the Haymarket and received the *Evening Standard* Award for the best comedy and the best new play in the Drama Awards for 1980. Two translations have been produced by the National Theatre, *The Cherry Orchard* and *The Fruits of Enlightenment.* He has written two plays for television—*Jamie on a Flying Visit* and *Birthday,* and a series called *Making Faces. Great Railway Journeys of the World* is the fourth film that he and Dennis Marks have collaborated on, the other three being *Imagine a City Called Berlin; Vienna: The Mask of Gold* and *Three Streets in the Country.*

LUDOVIC KENNEDY is best known for his numerous television appearances in current affairs and other programmes during the last twenty-five years. At present he chairs *Did You See...?,* the programme that discusses other television programmes, on BBC2. As a writer he has made a reputation for books about miscarriages of justice, such as *10 Rillington Place* and *Wicked Beyond Belief,* and on naval affairs such as *Pursuit,* about the chase and sinking of the *Bismarck.* He has loved trains since he can remember: his recent, best-selling anthology, *A Book of Railway Journeys,* reflects this.

MILES KINGTON was born in Northern Ireland in 1941 and spent the rest of his youth in North Wales, though he has neither Welsh nor Irish blood. He lived as a boy at Gresford near Wrexham, on the Great Western Railway, and spent five years night and day watching trains go by, which seemed to him all the education anyone needed. His parents disagreed and sent him to school in Northern Scotland, fifteen miles from the nearest train. He has a little Scottish blood.

After studying French and German at Oxford, he became a journalist. He has worked for ten years as jazz critic of *The Times,* for twelve years on the staff of Punch and for ten years in the musical group Instant Sunshine; luckily these functions largely overlapped, otherwise he would now be nearly sixty. Among his publications are *The World of Alphonse Allais* and *Let's Parler Franglais!* He now lives in Notting Hill near Paddington Station, HQ of GWR, though this a coincidence, not a childhood hang-up.

MICHAEL PALIN was born in Sheffield when it still had two passenger stations. He began to collect train numbers wherever his pram was parked, but, thwarted in his ambition to become a full-time train-spotter, he instead made do with a hastily assembled writing and performing act which he called 'Michael Palin'. Launched on regional TV in Bristol in 1965, it continued against all advice through *The Frost Report, Do Not Adjust Your Set, Monty Python, Ripping Yarns, Jabberwocky* and *Time Bandits* films, coming to a halt (believed to be Kyle of Lochalsh) with *Great Railway Journeys of the World.*

ERIC ROBSON was born in Newcastleton in the Scottish borders. His grandfather was a stationmaster on the Waverley line. He joined ITV in Carlisle first as a clerk and then as a studio floor manager. He's been a free-lance writer and reporter working mainly for the BBC for six years. The presenter of *Brass Tacks* on BBC 2 and a regular reporter on the Radio 4 *File on 4* programme he also commentates on outside broadcasts such as the State Opening of Parliament and the Lord Mayor's Show, and presents programmes throughout the year for BBC Newcastle.

BRIAN THOMPSON is a playwright and novelist. He has lived in Yorkshire since 1961, and has some experience of documentary television through his long association with BBC TV NORTH, for whom he has written many half-hour features reflecting regional life. Three of these have won awards. His first novel, *Buddy Boy,* was well received by critics and was a runner-up for the Guardian Fiction Prize. It was followed by a novel for children, *Trooper Jackson's Story.* As well as many single plays for television and radio, he has written three plays for the stage, all of them originally produced at the Stephen Joseph Theatre in the Round at Scarborough, under the direction of Alan Ayckbourn. They are *Patriotic Bunting, Tishoo,* and *The Conservatory.* Of these, *Tishoo* was transferred to the West End, with Alec McCowen and Penelope Wilton starring.

MICHAEL WOOD was born in Manchester and educated at Manchester Grammar School and at Oriel College, Oxford, where he read Modern History. He held undergraduate and postgraduate scholarships and in 1972 won the University's English Essay prize. His research work was in tenth-century history. Since 1976 he has worked for the BBC. He wrote and presented the 'In Search of...'series and has written a book based on the programmes called *In Search of the Dark Ages.* Among his forthcoming publications is a full-length study of King Athelstan and his age.

INDEX

181